The Atlantic Celts

Ancient People or Modern Invention?

The Atlantic
CELTS

Ancient People or Modern Invention?

Simon James

BRITISH MUSEUM PRESS

For Patsy and Alan

© Simon James 1999
Published by British Museum Press
A division of The British Museum Company Ltd
46 Bloomsbury Street, London WC1B 3QQ

First published 1999
Fourth impression 2000

Simon James has asserted his right to be identified as the Author of this Work

British Library Cataloguing in Publication Data
A catalogue record for this book is available from the British Library
ISBN 0-7141-2165-7

Designed and typeset in Photina by Martin Richards
Cover design by Slatter-Anderson
Printed in Great Britain by
The Bath Press, Bath

Contents

PREFACE

I n a synthesis such as this, most of the content is drawn from the work of many archaeologists and academics working in other fields. Of particular importance in prompting my interest in the whole area has been the work of a number of Iron Age specialists, notably J.D. Hill, while the recent book on archaeology and ethnicity by Siân Jones was crucial to the present essay (especially chapters 3 and 4). I am also very grateful to a number of colleagues in Durham University Department of Archaeology, in particular Sam Lucy, Pam Graves and Margarita Díaz-Andreu for letting me sit in on their fascinating course on the archaeology of identity during 1997-8. I should also like to thank John Collis for information, Nicola Terrenato for ideas about pre-Roman Italy, Jo Story for information on Saxon England, and Pam Graves for valuable observations about Scottish identity. Colin Haselgrove, Catherine Johns, Sam Lucy, Annie Matonis, Martin Millett, Tim Potter, Jonathan Williams and Sue Youngs provided valuable comments on all or parts of the text. I should also especially like to thank Teresa Francis and Emma Way at British Museum Press. It is conventional, but in the present case perhaps more than usually important, to emphasize that none of the above necessarily agree with the ideas or conclusions presented in this book, or are responsible for what I may have made of their thoughts.

Simon James
Durham, November 1998

Shetland Islands

Orkney Islands

ATLANTIC OCEAN

Hebrides

North West Highlands

Grampians

Scotland

Edinburgh

Southern Uplands

NORTH SEA

Northern
Ireland

Belfast

Pennines

Isle of Man

Republic of
Ireland

IRISH SEA

Dublin

Cambrian Mountains

England

Wales

Cardiff

London

Cornwall

0   100 miles

0   160 kilometres

ENGLISH CHANNEL

INTRODUCTION

I occupy a fascinating, if sometimes rather precarious position between several worlds: those of university archaeology departments, museums and the kaleidoscope of diverse groups which go to make up the 'general public' in Britain. As an archaeologist who has worked for over a decade as an educator in the British Museum, I have long been concerned to try to build bridges between these all too often mutually uncomprehending worlds, through talking and writing. In my own fields of academic interest – especially Roman and Iron Age studies in Britain – I find myself living in an extremely exciting phase of development. These disciplines are still in the midst of ground-breaking revolutions in which all the old certainties are crumbling. For some decades, the pace of change has been gathering speed, culminating in a radical reformulation of ideas about history, and especially how we conceptualize vanished human societies. One of the consequences of this shift has been the widespread abandonment of the idea that the pre-Roman centuries in Britain and Ireland (and perhaps elsewhere) should be thought of as Celtic.

Celtic culture in Britain and Ireland is still widely believed to find its genesis and initial expression in the last millennium BC, during the Iron Age. Recently, vast quantities of new archaeological evidence have been gathered from this period of insular prehistory and very different approaches developed to understanding what it can tell us – not least from anthropological research on how societies other than our own urban industrial world actually work. This has completely undermined the received picture of early Celtic societies. In consequence, we have been asking where the idea of the 'insular Celts' came from in the first

1. *Ireland and Britain in the later twentieth century, a map which, politically, may soon change again, as it has so many times before. Stippled areas indicate land over 600 ft (183 m).*

place. It has absolutely no ancient pedigree: it is a modern interpretation, not unambiguous historical truth.

During the early 1990s, I spent much time discussing the pre-Roman past with people in the British Museum's galleries, surrounded by famous treasures and everyday remains of the vanished societies of early Britain, Ireland and continental Europe. These conversations made me increasingly aware of a chronic problem: a widening gap of comprehension between the ways in which most people in Ireland and Britain understand their remote past, and the ideas archaeologists now hold about it. In particular, I became intrigued by the continued prevalence of belief in a Celtic Antiquity for Britain, given the extent of its academic discrediting among most (but not all) of those who work on the period. Many archaeologists now see it as a dangerously misleading anachronism which, far from helping us understand remote times, seriously falsifies our history. It seems to me remarkable that something which touches on the very foundations of 'our accepted, shared national histories in these islands should have made so little impact outside the academic world. Clearly, there is a major task of explanation to be undertaken.

The issue is all the more important since in this case, unusually for Britain especially, the work of archaeologists obviously has profound political implications. As the most important constitutional changes for generations affect the constituent states, the peoples of the islands are enduring the most intensive period in living memory of soul-searching about their separate and shared identities and the very labels they should use to describe themselves, each other, and the islands on which they live (fig. 1). For example, some, especially in Ireland, now object to terms such as 'British Isles' (although in the absence of agreed alternatives it is still used in this book, as are neutral terms such as 'the islands'; another alternative, 'Atlantic archipelago', has detractors of its own). May 1999 sees the inauguration of the new Scottish Parliament and Welsh Assembly, at a time when (we fervently hope) Ireland, too, is painfully feeling its way at last towards a new rapprochement between its warring communities. This is not only about finding long-term accommodations between old antagonists; equally important is incorporation of the major new, very different 'ethnic' communities, largely from former colonies.

It is part of a wider European phenomenon, perhaps the most dramatic and alarming manifestation of which has been the reawakening of dormant nationalisms across Europe, most disruptively in the East following the collapse of the Soviet Bloc. It is also evident in the West, as the component identities of a number of composite modern nation-states have acquired renewed self-consciousness and aspirations, most notably in Belgium, Italy and Spain, as well as in the British Isles. Another fundamental new factor is the European Union and the possibility of a federal European identity being added to the picture.

Negotiation of new cultural and political relationships depends on passionately held beliefs about identity, origins and history. As we rewrite constitutions, perhaps dissolving old bonds and creating new ones, it becomes an urgent task to examine frankly the historical assumptions on which our actions must be based. If the Ancient Celts of Britain and Ireland are an essentially bogus recent invention, what does this mean for modern people who regard themselves as Celts? If there is substance to the challenge, it does more than overturn conventional history: it would seem to undermine the entire basis of national and ethnic identities in Britain. Are the Ancient Celts of the isles just a romantic fantasy? And are the modern Celts therefore fake, even a dangerous political 'con' in the hands of separatists? Northern Ireland has graphically illustrated how senses of identity and partisan views of history may lead beyond controversy to violence. Or are the archaeologists concerned themselves driven by dark political motives, as some have alleged? In this brief work I hope to outline the arguments, and the implications, of this fascinating debate.

Agreed national histories are inevitably nationalist histories, and are always partisan. Many notions of deep history underpin ancient claims to territory and precedence over other groups, justify modern antagonisms and constitute the fault-lines of future conflict. There has been, of late, a resurgence of regional nationalisms throughout the British Isles, notably in Scotland and Wales, and this is likely to reawaken nationalist feelings in England too. Clear signs of narrow chauvinism are to be seen in some quarters in all these countries (not least in some English national newspapers), while for decades internecine hatreds have seen slaughter on the streets of Northern Ireland, sometimes spilling into other parts of the islands. With militant nationalism, and even genocide, resurgent nightmares in Eastern Europe, the potential dangers of letting nationalist sentiments – and prejudices – run unchallenged are all too obvious. Such ideologies depend on particular conceptions of history, in this case of how we, the peoples of the islands, came to be as we are. Such claims and assumptions must be as open to critical examination and debate as the policies of political parties, for history, like politics, is a field of interpretation and opinion, although not one of absolute relativism.

In writing this book I have a number of convergent purposes in mind. I have long been committed to communicating the fascination of archaeology, and of the European Iron Age and Roman worlds in particular, to the wider public. I have written two previous works relating to the Celts. The first, *Exploring the World of the Celts* (1993), was a general treatment of the entire 'Celtic world' written in the traditional mode. However, producing it left me with a growing conviction that the Celts, as popularly conceived, did not really exist, although what conception of the past might be offered in their place was not immediately apparent. Reading and talking to other archaeologists led me to the iconoclastic work of British Iron Age scholars such as J.D. Hill; and as I completed my first book, I was also introduced to a volume by the anthropologist Malcolm Chapman, *The Celts: The Construction of a Myth* (1992), a controversial work which deserves to be more widely known and which first opened my eyes to the nature and historical context of modern Celtic historiography. Meanwhile, John Collis has been one of the few archaeologists to enter the public fray on this issue, producing some highly provocative critiques of traditional views of the Celts. All this precipitated a profound shift in the way I see the pre-Roman past, a changed perspective which is to be seen in a further book, co-written with Valery Rigby, *Britain and the Celtic Iron Age* (1997). The present volume aims to explore the development of ideas about the Celts in their wider historical contexts.

Following these books, and other forays into print over Celtic issues (e.g. James 1998), I was invited by British Museum Press to write a short book to coincide with the first elections to the new Scottish Parliament and Welsh Assembly, which provides an opportune moment to raise some issues about insular Celtic identity, to pose some questions and to offer a preliminary sketch of some answers. This book is an essay, in the literal sense of an *attempt* at dissecting the history of the issue and formulating and presenting a very different view of the insular past. It is very much a snapshot of work in progress, and not a complete story.

It is the responsibility of those engaged in the historical sciences to contribute to debates which draw on historically rooted ideas, especially where they can see that the assumptions on which everyone is operating in the modern political world are false. To date, with some honourable exceptions, few archaeologists have shown much interest in talking to outsiders about the wider implications of research on the Iron Age, through pressure of work or disinclination to put their heads over the parapet. In my own experience some archaeologists can be unthinkingly contemptuous when asked quite reasonable questions by non-specialists, responding with dismissive 'how can you be so stupid?' answers to queries predicated on 'old' ideas like Ancient Celts. In this book, I hope to tackle the task of communicating ideas across the 'academic'/'popular' boundary, in both directions. For archaeologists have a duty to communicate, and much to learn from other academic and public groups, not least that they cannot just dismiss the Celtic issue and wash their hands.

This book, then, is aimed at two major audiences. Firstly, it is intended for the interested 'lay reader', as an attempt to explain how and why the academic world, past and present, has dealt with the issue of the Celts. It is equally aimed at fellow archaeologists and other specialists, in attempting to show that neither side of the debate consists of romantic fools or politically motivated knaves. The acceptance of mutual good faith among all interested parties, and an effort at greater open-mindedness, creates the possibility of constructive advance, even if consensus is neither likely nor necessary.

There are a number of particular role-models I have had in mind in attempting a book such as this. One is the leading British Iron Age archaeologist Barry Cunliffe. He is himself quite out of sympathy with the kind of approach presented here, and has disparaged much work in this area, recently dismissing it as 'politically correct' (Cunliffe 1997, pp. 19, 276). However, his commitment to, and skill in, public communication of archaeology remains an example unsurpassed in the present generation. My most important inspiration, however, is not an archaeologist at all, but an evolutionary biologist, Stephen Jay Gould. In his books and essays, Gould boldly tackles the most complex scientific issues in a way that any thinking person can comprehend:

The rules are simple: no compromises with conceptual richness; no bypassing of ambiguity or ignorance; removal of jargon, of course, but no dumbing down of ideas (any conceptual complexity can be conveyed in ordinary English).

(Gould 1991, p. 12)

2. *Europe as seen from the Atlantic archipelago. The conventional map of Europe (fig. 5) shows Ireland and Britain as peripheral to the continental land-mass, but to the people who have dwelt there, the islands have of course been central to their own universe. To greatly varying degrees, their inhabitants have looked inwards, towards each other, or outwards, across the seas towards adjacent peoples.*

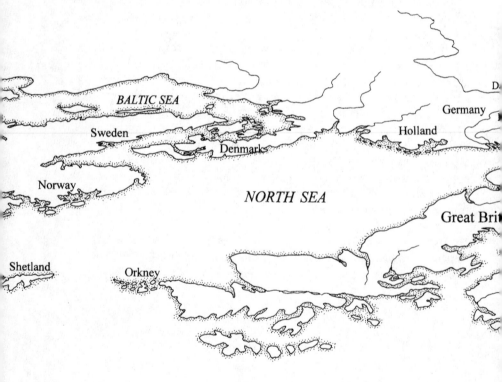

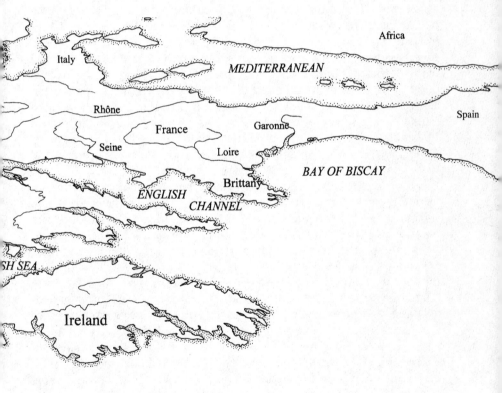

1 THE DEBATE ON CELTIC IDENTITY

It comes as a shock to an archaeologist accustomed to quietly pondering artefacts and monuments, and to talking in museum galleries and lecture rooms about the societies which made them, to be accused of 'ethnic cleansing' and even 'genocide'. These sharp responses were evoked by the work of Iron Age archaeologists in Britain especially, most of whom have come to the conclusion that our established belief that these islands, like much of continental Europe, were occupied by Celts in later prehistory, is simply wrong: the insular Ancient Celts never existed. At the moment this rejection of the Celts is not generally shared by specialists in other fields, or by many archaeologists outside the United Kingdom, and is fiercely opposed by some. The accusation that it amounts to a kind of ethnic cleansing comes from a swingeing general attack by Ruth and Vincent Megaw in a recent academic journal; that of 'genocide' was made against me personally, in a private response from a member of the public to the ideas on this subject presented on my own web-pages.

Such violent reactions show the deeply emotive character of human identities and the stakes involved in critically examining their nature and origins. For, of course, the idea of Celticness is still of great cultural and political importance, and a presumption of deep roots, of unbroken traditions and 'spirit' going back over 2,000 years to the pre-Roman centuries, is a fundamental feature of Celtic culture. When archaeologists, in seeking to understand the remote past, unexpectedly expose to critique the foundations of a modern ethnic or national identity, they are understandably seen as threatening people's fundamental beliefs about themselves and their world. To demolish the Ancient Celts of the isles is automatically perceived as an attack on modern Celtic identity as well. Archaeologists suddenly find themselves in the political spotlight, their own motivation open to suspicion. This book seeks to set out the whole question of the Celts of the isles, ancient and modern, and to look at the evidence, ideas and issues.

In these islands, our early history is something that many of us think little about, after our primary school encounters with 'cave men', Ancient Celtic Britons and Irish, Romans, Picts and Scots, Anglo-Saxons and Vikings. But to many others, the prehistoric Celtic element of this story has a special place at the root of their sense of identity. For almost everyone, the early past is not in itself contentious; we *know* its shape, the familiar foundation on which is built the modern conception of our national self-images and mutual relationships. Today no national or ethnic group calls itself 'the Celts' as its primary name, but, in the eyes of many, 'Celticness' is the shared, deeply ancient and highly characteristic cultural inheritance of several modern nations or peoples. The Celtic roots, tradition and living spirit of the Irish, Welsh, Scots, Cornish, Manx and Bretons are widely taken for granted. Celticness, then, is a major, but largely implicit, conceptual foundation, an essential part of the cultural bedrock of several societies, and their historical legacy to the wider world.

But there is powerful reason to assert that the outlines of early history on which *all* such national/ethnic origin stories rely are serious misrepresentations of the past; and that the example of the Celts of Atlantic Europe is one such case (although by no means the only one, as we shall see). For the evidence seems quite clear that *no one in Britain or Ireland called themselves a 'Celt' or 'Celtic' before 1700*. A woman living at Maiden Castle hillfort in Dorset during the fourth century BC, a pagan priest at Navan, Ireland, in the second century BC, a monk on Iona 800 years later, a child at the court of Hywel Dda in 950, or a Highland clansman driving cattle in sixteenth-century Scotland, would all have been puzzled to hear themselves called Celts.

Of course, the terms 'Celt' and 'Celtic' were used in Antiquity, by Greek and Roman authors to describe certain 'barbarian' neighbours and in less certain ways by some such peoples of themselves. But they were used strictly of continental peoples; the islanders had different names. In the context of the isles, the term 'Celtic' is a modern coining, not a truth handed down directly from generation to generation from the remote past. The Welsh, Scots, Irish and other peoples have only come to describe themselves and their ancestors as Celts since the eighteenth century. The notion of insular Celts, past and present, then, is a modern interpretation and an adopted 'ethnonym' (i.e. an ethnic group's name for itself).

Many might respond that, even if the name itself is a recent application and was never a true ethnonym in the past, it nevertheless remains a valid and useful *cultural* label which we may apply to earlier insular peoples (who were *in essence* the same as each other) as well as to the historically attested peoples called Celts in continental Europe. I shall argue that this position cannot be sustained either, partly because we are so used to equating the notion of 'cultures' with 'peoples' that 'Celtic' as a cultural label quickly elides back into an ethnic one. Moreover, similarities of original languages, which undoubtedly existed and which are taken as the most fundamental evidence for the cultural oneness of the insular Celtic peoples, are not determinants either of particular cultural affiliation or of common genealogical descent. Indeed, as we shall see, the very naming of these languages as 'Celtic' around 1700 was no inevitable choice, but depended on assumptions about early history and the supposed prehistoric movements of named peoples. Using these language classifications to write history then creates a danger of circular argument.

But more fundamentally, this 'cultural' reading is challenged because there are reasons to believe that the whole idea of an essentially uniform *'culture* we can call Celtic' spanning early Europe is as much a modern, artificial construct as the notion of people actually called Celts in early Britain and Ireland. Certainly in the context of the isles, and it might be argued in the case of Europe as a whole, the idea of 'Celts' is so laden with historical baggage and political distortion that, with regard to the past at least, we must drop the term entirely if we are to get any closer to understanding the peoples of Iron Age Europe.

Such, then, is the challenge posed in this book to conventional notions of ancient insular history. Are they the discovery of a profound ancient reality, which we can see from our vantage point in the late twentieth century, while the peoples of the past themselves did not see it? Or is the idea of Ancient Celts in the British Isles an unwarranted anachronism, a modern academic, political and cultural fiction thrust onto the past, distorting it until its true shape is unrecognizable? If it is a fiction, does this mean that modern Celtic identity is a fraud as well?

THE CELTS OF THE ISLANDS

Everyone who grows up in Britain or Ireland learns that the remote past of the islands was, and much of its present still is, in some sense Celtic. The idea that there were, and are, Celtic peoples in Britain and Ireland is a key element of the shared national histories of the peoples of Europe's Atlantic archipelago.

The modern Celtic peoples live on what Barry Cunliffe has elegantly called the 'Atlantic façade' of Europe, down the western side of the British Isles and on the adjacent fringes of continental Europe, in Brittany (some would also include Galicia in Spain). I refer to the peoples in question as the 'Atlantic Celts' to distinguish them from the wider family of vanished peoples known as Celts who, over 2,000 years ago, are believed to have lived right across Europe and into modern Turkey. Other European countries have their own cultural traditions about, and political uses for, the Ancient Celts: the French traditionally regard themselves as direct descendants of the powerful Celtic Gauls (see below). In Spain, too, Ancient Celts have been incorporated into nationalist histories and ideologies. Recent years have seen yet another political use for the Celts, as the pan-European prehistoric forerunners of the European Union: such was the message of the major exhibition *I Celti* held in Venice in 1991. This creates an interesting paradox in that while, in Britain and Ireland, notions of Celticness are about cultural boundaries and distinctiveness (especially difference from the English), on the continent they may be about European solidarity and integration. But in continental Europe the idea of *living* cultural 'Celticity' is largely confined to Brittany. (The latter region will not be discussed in any detail, as its story is more intimately related to that of France and it has not been a major player in the political and cultural history of the isles since the eighteenth century, which is the main focus of this book.)

Another reason for speaking of 'Atlantic Celts' is that millions of people who claim ancestry in these homelands now live on the other side of that same ocean; to be sure, great numbers went even further afield, not least to Australasia, but the majority are in the Americas. Some are in South America (for example, a Welsh community in Argentine Patagonia), but most are in the United States – most famously the American Irish – and in Canada, where dwell communities of Scottish origin, by whom the culture and language of the Highlands are jealously guarded. That these millions in the lands of the 'Celtic diaspora' claim such descent makes the history of the Atlantic Celts a global concern, not just a European one.

But who were the Ancient Celts, and who are the modern Celts? Because of the deep antiquity which is attached to it, the name 'Celtic' conjures up in people's minds a bewildering variety of images.

IMAGES OF CELTICNESS

Everyone knows, at some level, what 'Celtic' means in the context of contemporary Ireland and Britain – it is part of popular culture. Hence journalists can refer to Ireland, booming in the 1990s, as the 'Celtic tiger economy' and know they will be understood. Today, within the Atlantic archipelago, 'Celtic' is used primarily of the non-English peoples of the isles who speak, or who until recent times spoke, languages of the Celtic family. Among those peoples, the term is used in varying ways – and by no means universally – of themselves, both collectively and more specifically; in Ireland, 'Celtic' is sometimes employed as a virtual synonym for 'indigenous Irish'. It should be noted that not everyone indigenous to the Celtic lands accepts or wants Celtic identity: many see it as uninteresting or irrelevant, and ignore or reject the label. The Celticness of Scotland is especially contentious, as according to traditional outlines of its history the kingdom arose from the union of several groups, including non-Celtic-speaking populations. Nevertheless, the term is widely used, if vaguely and haphazardly. Wider still are its meanings in the context of history.

'Celtic' is sometimes used as a general adjective for almost anything to do with the distant insular past. For some, especially New Age romantics and mystics, Ancient Celts may be rooted in a remote ahistorical dreamtime, evoked especially by earthwork monuments and standing stones which were actually erected 1,000, even 3,000, years before the name 'Celt' is encountered anywhere. But for many others, there are much more specific associations: most historical visions of the Celts trace their point of departure deep in the Iron Age prehistory of Europe, when people called Celts first appear in historical records.

These earliest known people called Celts lived in continental Europe, and seem to be attested in regions north of the Alps and near the Pyrenees during the sixth century BC. They apparently expanded by migrations south and east, and are widely believed to have invaded Britain and Ireland, establishing a vast 'Celtic commonwealth' (some even call it a 'Celtic empire') stretching from the Atlantic to central Turkey. T. G. E. Powell, in his book *The Celts*, published in 1958 and still in print, called them the 'first great nation north of the Alps whose name we know'.

The earliest Celts are widely seen, then, as in essence a single people, or a group of intimately related peoples – societies which shared related languages of the Celtic family and which were characterized by common values, social organization and arts. Many consider that these aspects are evidence of an underlying cultural unity and a distinctive shared 'Celtic spirit', which has lasted unbroken and unchanging from ancient to modern times. This essentially timeless Celticity is valued as forming a seamless link between the Ancient Britons and Irish of the Iron Age and the peoples of modern Wales, Scotland, Ireland and other areas such as Cornwall. Today, this continuity of 'spirit' still marks out the Celtic peoples as distinctly different from their more numerous English neighbours. Thus the Celts claim a pedigree which makes them one of the most ancient of all the living ethnic or national groups of Europe, having maintained their identity for over 2,500 years.

The Celts are seen as once 'heroic' warrior societies, based on classical descriptions of the Gauls and early Irish accounts which describe feasting and hard drinking, a love of adornment and eloquence, boasting, duelling, battle and, in earliest times, head-hunting. Such figures as Cú Chulainn, hero of ancient Irish epic, are seen as wild but noble, romantic and fearless free spirits, an image drawn on by modern films such as *Highlander*, *Rob Roy* and *Braveheart*. (The unhappy mirror image of this is the very negative modern stereotype of the unruly, violent and drunken Scot or Irishman.)

'Celtic' also has some specific but highly divergent religious connotations: of pagan cult, especially Druidism, with spurious further associations with the standing stones of a much earlier period. The Druids fascinate through their supposed intimacy with nature: the word 'Druid' is related to the Celtic root for 'oak', and Druidic rites are associated with forest groves and the cutting of mistletoe. Druids are also believed to have been deeply versed in cosmology and the ways of the gods. The will of the latter could be divined, and their wrath perhaps averted, through human sacrifice, which is an additional source of horrified fascination and frisson today.

There is a second, very different religious association of the term. 'Celtic' has become attached to a particular brand of early Christianity, the Irish-centred Church of the post-Roman centuries. The monks and clergy of the early Celtic Church are justly celebrated today, not only for the piety and zeal of the Irish, and Irish-trained, missionaries who took Christianity to so many pagan peoples (not least the English), but also for the illuminated gospel books which still today bear witness to their devotion and artistic talents.

The complex borders and elaborated initial letters, the knotwork and stylized animals which spill in brilliant colours across the pages of these early manuscripts are widely seen as a late manifestation of 'Celtic art'. It is a term which is rarely defined very specifically, but primarily refers to artefacts designed and embellished in what archaeologists and art historians call 'La Tène style'. This arose in Central Europe during the fifth century BC, inspiring a range of derivative styles and motifs traceable far into the Roman imperial period and beyond. Best known on metalwork of the pre-Roman Iron Age (where it swirls across weapons, jewellery and the trappings of horses and wheeled vehicles), it consists mostly of abstract, geometric patterns, many of which are devolved plant and flower designs, sometimes incorporating stylized animals or human faces. Some elements, such as the three-fold whirligig or *triskele*, are still to be seen in the Irish Christian manuscripts of the eighth century AD.

Early Christian clerics in Ireland and Britain also helped to ensure the survival of evidence of vernacular language and oral literature by writing them down for the first time. It is due to the establishment of literacy that we know in detail the Celtic languages of the early Middle Ages. From these same sources, we also have precious ancient legends and tales such as the *Ulster Cycle* and the *Mabinogion* and the roots of the legend of Arthur.

Although many traditions, such as the bardic tradition in Wales, were broken in recent centuries, nonetheless there was considerable continuity of culture and language which, with the direct survivals of ancient art and literature, helped form the basis for the 'Celtic revival' of recent generations, as the peoples of the isles each developed a stronger sense of national self-consciousness.

As we shall see, this self-consciousness began with a new awareness of the importance of indigenous languages, which were already under threat from the spread of English (Cornish became extinct in the eighteenth century). Preservation and enhancement of the status of Celtic tongues, and the maintenance and development of the rich literary traditions of these regions expressed either in Celtic or English, have been major features of recent generations. From events such as the Welsh *Eisteddfodau* to the international reputations of Irish, Scottish and Welsh writers and poets, there is a sense of continuity of a particular sensibility tangibly different from that of English writers.

Around the world, perhaps the most widely appreciated modern manifestation of Celtic cultural traditions is music, both for its inherent qualities and because language is no barrier to its appreciation. Ireland and

3. Oliver Sheppard's statue of Cú Chulainn, depicting the death of the young Celtic warrior hero of pre-Christian Irish epic. The statue was selected as an appropriate monument to the Nationalist martyrs of the rising of Easter 1916, and today stands in the General Post Office in Dublin, the major focus of the fighting.

Scotland, in particular, possess musical traditions unbroken for centuries, which continue to be appreciated and which have inspired many other musical fields, not least in North America. 'Celtic music' is also a significant strand in contemporary musical genres, from rock to New Age.

Usually less overt, but widely and deeply felt, is the political significance of a sense of living Celticness, of profound connection with the distant past. For many, the idea of ancient Celtic cultural roots forms the essential pre-existing, transnational, cultural substrate on which are built the ethnic and political identities of the Welsh, Scots, Irish and others. It is rarely stressed today (especially at a time when, for instance, nationalists in Wales need votes from all parts of the nation), but is always there. A perhaps startling illustration of this is to be found in the General Post Office in Dublin. Inside stands a statue commemorating the tragedy of the 1916 Easter Rising of Irish nationalists against British rule (fig. 3). It

4. *The paradoxes and contradictions of the past: a loyalist mural in East Belfast, photographed in 1993, in which Cú Chulainn is claimed as a hero of Protestant Ulster. In the legends he was, after all, a man of Ulster who died defending his land against other Irishmen. Represented as the forerunner of the present illegal loyalist paramilitary group, the Ulster Defence Association, the image of the ancient hero is ironically, or provocatively, taken from the nationalist monument in Dublin (fig. 3).*

consists of a bare-limbed youth hanging dead on a tree. But in Catholic Ireland, this is not Christ on the cross, but the legendary ancient Irish warrior-hero, Cú Chulainn, a memory of pre-Christian, Iron Age times. While I was photographing the statue some years ago, an elderly woman stopped and rubbed his foot. She explained that it was for luck; she had just bought her national lottery ticket. I noticed the projecting foot was brightly polished from such devotions. The pagan Celtic past is still powerful in Ireland. Indeed, the idea of an ancient Celtic origin for Irishness was of growing importance to Irish nationalists during the nineteenth century, and has continued to be part of the ideological foundations of the nation ever since – so much so, that senior Irish archaeologists who now doubt the validity of the idea still find it too sensitive to discuss openly. The continued profound significance in Irish nationalism of that distant past is also to be seen in the response of some Northern Irish Protestants, who are themselves staking a bid to a share of that past: they have adopted Cú Chulainn as a symbol of their own, on the grounds that he was an Ulsterman who defended his country against 'Irish attacks' (fig. 4), and some are learning the Irish language themselves. The war of identities in Ireland is now being fought out in the Celtic past, too.

Celticness is a living political, as well as a cultural issue, which is why it is important to discuss it, and so crucial to examine it rigorously. The starting point for me is where my own field, archaeology, intersects with Celticness, in the established histories of Celtic origins on which modern conceptions of Celticness are largely built.

2 STANDARD HISTORIES:
ASSUMPTIONS, LIMITATIONS
AND OBJECTIONS

Just as there are innumerable conceptions of the insular Celts, so there are many versions of their history. By no means everyone would subscribe to the 'canonical' account presented here, but versions more or less like it are commonly to be found in popular books and on numerous web-sites. It is obviously a vast simplification, but represents the kind of thumbnail sketch most of us have as our model of the history of a particular region or people.

Such mainstream models of Celtic history see the insular Celtic peoples as being related to the Gauls and other continental Celts of the first millennium BC; indeed, they have long been thought of as invading and migrant populations, arriving during the Iron Age (fig. 5). The apparent similarities and connections between continental and insular Celts have long been emphasized, in language, art, religion, warfare and social customs, and settlements. Hillforts, particular types of arms and jewellery, and patterns of decoration seem to bespeak a prehistoric Celtic commonwealth stretching from Scotland to Portugal and Turkey. This is an elaborately documented, well-established view of the past, widely regarded as the foundation for modern Celtic identities.

The first known Celts

By around 800–600 BC, in the lands just north of the Alps, peoples had appeared whom their literate Greek neighbours to the south came to call *Keltoi*, the first time we encounter their name. Around the same time, Celts are attested in Spain too. Because they were non-literate, we have no accounts written by themselves; these were therefore still 'prehistoric' peoples, although their societies were evidently sophisticated and technologically skilled. Iron-working had recently

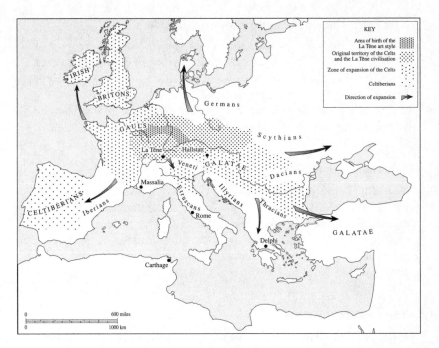

5. *How the later prehistoric 'Celtic world' has often been envisaged during the twentieth century, with migration in almost all directions from a supposed original 'homeland' in central Europe. (Based on Megaw and Megaw 1989, fig. 2.)*

been introduced, hence archaeologists call this last phase of European prehistory the 'Iron Age'. These earliest-known Celts formed principalities which traded with the Greeks and Etruscans. Around 500 BC the rich hillforts at the centres of these principalities were violently destroyed.

During the fifth century BC, in a band of territory stretching across Europe from eastern France through Germany, Austria and into Bohemia, new groups arose, characterized by, among other things, particular types of graves (including those of warriors) and a new kind of art. Archaeologists have given the name 'La Tène culture' to the physical remains of these groups who, around 400 BC, suddenly erupted into Italy and began to settle in the Po Valley.

The Celtic Gauls: fearsome barbarian invaders

These were the ancient continental Celts *par excellence*, otherwise known as Gauls (*Galli* in Latin). No longer a distant curiosity for Greek travellers and scholars, the Celts were suddenly a fearsome and immediate 'barbarian' danger. Around 390 BC, the Gallic *Senones* sacked Rome itself, but were driven back and largely contained beyond the Apennines, in the Po Valley which to the Romans became *Gallia Cisalpina*, 'Gaul this side of the Alps'.

The Galatians of Turkey

Migrating Celtic groups also invaded the Balkans and, in 279 BC, attacked Delphi, the greatest shrine in Greece. Beaten back with terrible losses, some nevertheless crossed into what is now Turkey and established a 'robber-kingdom' around modern Ankara. Known by the Greek equivalent of the Roman name 'Gauls', these *Galatae* gave their name to the land, Galatia, and so to the Galatians of the New Testament.

The Celts in the West

It has also long been assumed that there were waves of Celts moving westwards and north-westwards from the Central European homeland, to match the historically attested Mediterranean migrations – even though there were no literate observers in these areas to record such invasions. Nonetheless, the Romans found people calling themselves Celtiberians in Spain, and there are traces of Celtic dialects in various parts of the Iberian peninsula. These have been explained as a result of early, unrecorded Celtic invasions.

Inferring Celtic invasions of Britain and Ireland

Likewise, it has long been believed that there were Celtic invasions of the islands. Caesar recorded that Gauls, especially *Belgae*, had settled in Britain. Identical tribal names are found on the continent and in Britain (e.g. *Atrebates*, *Parisi*). Modern language studies have shown that the indigenous tongues of the British and the Irish are closely related to that of the ancient continental Gauls; they are all members of the Celtic family of languages. As archaeology developed, the artefacts characteristic of Iron Age Britain and Ireland began to be identified, and revealed important links with the world of the continental Celtic

Gauls: all three groupings produced the same kind of characteristic La Tène-style 'Celtic' art with swirling lines, suggesting vegetation, and perhaps stylized faces of people and animals. There seemed to be a common emphasis on weapons, strongholds and warfare, and historical documents suggested institutions in common, too, not least in religion – Druids, for example, are attested amongst all three groups.

The Ancient British and Irish, then, came to be seen as Celts like the Gauls and related continental peoples from Spain to Turkey. Further, the available evidence was assumed to mean that they arrived as waves of invaders, mostly or entirely during the Iron Age.

Iron Age Celtic society

All these Iron Age societies, from Ireland to Galatia, tend to be seen as variations on a well-defined conception of a typical Celtic society. This is usually envisaged as possessing a characteristic social organization (with a social hierarchy including specialized classes of aristocratic warriors, Druids and other priests, and privileged people with specialist skills, such as bards and smiths) and exhibiting characteristic cultural traits, including, centrally, Celtic language, rich oral traditions (of oratory and literature), music and material arts. Such societies tended to bellicosity, but this is often seen as reflecting fierce independence and pride, which extended to women as well, in a way which shocked the Graeco-Roman world. They were also deeply religious, their beliefs and cults focusing especially on natural places such as woodland groves, pools and water-courses. 'Celtic spirit' is perhaps best exemplified in the Celtic love of both feasting and religious observances.

Roman conquest: destruction of continental 'Celtdom'

During the last three centuries BC, the expanding Roman empire gradually subjugated all of the continental Celtic world, except for areas north of the Rhine and Danube, which were soon overrun by another group of 'barbarian' peoples, the early Germans.

Many of the wholly or partly Celtic areas, such as the 'Three Gauls' (roughly modern France and the Rhineland) and Hispania (Spain and Portugal), became prosperous Roman provinces, but Celtic language and lifestyle did not survive the process of 'Romanization'. All these lands came to speak Latin dialects, ancestral to the 'Romance' languages of today (Spanish, French, Portuguese, Catalan, etc.). Rome all but extinguished 'Celticity' on the European mainland.

Britain, Ireland and Rome

In Britain, Roman occupation of, roughly, the lands which would one day be England and Wales led to a similar loss of Celtic language and culture in the east of the island, although it proved more tenacious in the west. And there was continuity of independence among the free 'barbarians' of Caledonia (northern Scotland), while Ireland was never invaded by Rome at all. (Drumanagh in County Dublin, a long known but little investigated site recently claimed to have been a Roman military base, was in fact almost certainly a trading centre.)

Picts and Scots

As the empire began to decay in the third and fourth centuries, the remnants of the free Celts moved onto the offensive. In Caledonia a new confederation, the Picts, appeared. These threatened the Roman frontier, while Irish sea-raiders, known as *Scotti*, raided the western coasts, even as Germanic Angles and Saxons were raiding the east.

Catastrophe for the Britons

In the fifth century AD Roman Britain collapsed, and the Anglo-Saxons invaded and settled the east, eventually to establish Germanic-speaking England. They pressed the native British groups, whom they called 'Welsh' ('strangers' or 'foreigners'), ever westwards, into the land which would become Wales and Cornwall.

The conquest of Brittany

From the west, some Britons crossed to Armorica, the western extremity of Gaul, even as that land was becoming France (after the name of its new Germanic overlords, the Franks). The British migrants were not so much refugees from Anglo-Saxon invasion as invaders themselves: many peoples were on the move at this time, and the Britons took this opportunity for some expansion of their own. Henceforth, the island of Britain was distinguished as 'great Britain' to avoid confusion with this new 'little Britain' (Brittany).

The Irish in Britain: the origin of Scotland

The Irish, too, joined in the military free-for-all, slave-raiding their fellow Celts in Britain (their most famous captive being, of course, the young St Patrick). They also settled in Britain, most importantly on the west coast of Scotland, which was to take its name from these settlers in Argyll; the land of these *Scotti* became *Scotia*. Eventually, wars with the Picts and other lesser kingdoms led to union as the historic kingdom of Scotland, in AD 843.

Ireland becomes the land of saints and scholars

Ireland itself became a Christian land as a result of the work of St Patrick in the fifth century, and became one of the greatest centres of piety and learning in Europe during the seventh and eighth centuries AD, its clerics and artists having a profound influence in Britain (not least among the English) and on the continent.

The Celts in medieval times and beyond

BRITTANY, an independent kingdom in the ninth century, became one of the various almost-independent duchies which made up medieval France. As central royal power grew in the fifteenth century, so Brittany's independence dwindled, and it was politically absorbed by France in 1532.

WALES remained a separate principality, but came under increasing English dominance from the tenth century. In 1485 the Welshman Henry Tudor became King of England, but his totally Anglicized son Henry VIII united Wales politically to England by Acts of Parliament between 1536 and 1543. Much of Welsh native culture disappeared in the sixteenth century with the abolition of Welsh law.

SCOTLAND was culturally divided, roughly, between the Gaelic (Irish Celtic, 'Erse') speakers of the Highlands and those who spoke Scots (a Germanic dialect, close to English) in the Lowlands. The warlike clans and chieftains of the Highlands were often in conflict with their Lowland neighbours, who thought them cattle-thieving barbarians. This formed the background to their eventual brutal suppression after their support (albeit equivocal) for the Catholic Bonnie Prince Charlie's attempt in 1745–6 to seize back from the Protestant Hanoverians the British throne for the ancient Scottish Royal House of Stewart.

IRELAND Once the Vikings began to raid in 795, Ireland was increasingly dominated, partly or wholly, by foreigners. The Vikings were followed by the Anglo-Normans in the twelfth century. During the sixteenth century the English colonial grip tightened, and relations were further embittered by the Reformation. Protestant England kept Catholic Ireland under subjugation, sometimes incredibly brutal. From 1800 until after the First World War, Ireland was a largely reluctant part of the United Kingdom.

THE GREAT MIGRATIONS All these lands saw substantial or massive migrations, especially from the eighteenth century onwards. Migrants were partly lured away from often terrible conditions and starvation on the land (culminating in the catastrophe of the Irish potato famine of the 1840s) to equally squalid, but more reliably paid, employment in the industrial cities of Britain, or to the promise of land and liberty in the Americas and Australasia. Many of them, especially in Ireland and Scotland, were unwilling to leave, but were driven away by lairds and landlords who put profits above the welfare of their own people.

The rediscovery of a common Celtic heritage

The eighteenth century saw the beginnings of nationalism in Ireland and elsewhere, and the rediscovery of a common Celtic heritage. The study of language, and the beginnings of archaeology, laid the foundation for more detailed understanding of the histories of these peoples, and contributed to growing national self-consciousness, exhibited in politics and in cultural forms, not least art and literature. Perhaps this process reached maturity with the establishment of an independent Irish state in 1921.

The Celts today: homelands and 'diaspora'

Today, the Celtic countries are undergoing a period of political and cultural renewal, with a wealthy and confident Irish Republic, hopes of constitutional rapprochement in Northern Ireland, and devolution in Wales and Scotland. In the lands of the diaspora and indeed around the globe, Celtic culture, not least music, enjoys great prestige and popularity.

It may be thought that a people should be best placed to know its own story, which will preserve traditions passed from generation to generation, learned at the grandparent's knee: outsiders question it at their peril. But there are very good reasons to challenge such a judgement, for *any* established, popular outline of ethnic or national history, and specifically in the case of the Celts. The claims of *all* such histories should be questioned and tested as a matter of course.

As we have seen, the startling reality is that no one in Britain or Ireland called themselves 'Celtic' or 'a Celt' (and no one applied such names to them either) until after 1700. No early Irish or Welsh source, nor any Greek or Roman author before them, ever calls the peoples of the isles 'Celts'. So can the outline of 'Celtic' history set out above possibly be valid?

THE NATURE OF HISTORY

History is fundamental to our sense of identity, but it is not 'what happened in the past', for the past is completely inaccessible to us. History is not *inherited*, handed down directly from generation to generation, a truthful, ready-made account unaltered thereafter. Nor do we *discover* history as unambiguous truth dictated by the surviving evidence of the past: rather, we *create* history. In the broadest sense – covering both document-based historical studies and material-based archaeology – history is the construction by modern minds of imagined (although not wholly imaginary!) pasts, from the fragmentary surviving debris of past societies. History is what *we* think, say and write about the evidence for the past. Inevitably, to a large degree it is governed by our prejudices. But this does not mean that absolutely anything goes; the evidence forms the all-important framework for, and places constraints on, the models of the past that we construct.

Historical information may come from folklore, surviving early writings or, in the case of archaeology, from physical traces left by vanished peoples. But all these sources are partial, in two senses of the word: they are inevitably incomplete selections of what happened and what existed, because of physical decay, forgetfulness or deliberate erasure at earlier stages. They are not impartial, either, since surviving verbal and written accounts were created by people with their own prejudices, and transmitted by others, perhaps equally partisan (whether through folk-tales or state histories). Archaeological evidence, too, suffers from analogous selections and transformations which may distort the picture. What survives is down to the quirky habits of people, who may or may not bury their dead or whose privileged groups are more likely to leave traces of their lives than the materially deprived poor. And these traces are prone to the selective processes of decay, which may preserve pots but not textiles.

Then there is our own direct contribution, in our ignorance or selectivity in identifying surviving sources of information, in our effectiveness at recovering them, in the value we place on them, and in the interpretations we derive from them. In writing histories, we select, emphasize or downplay according to our own views and prejudices. This should come as no surprise, since we cannot agree on how our own, directly experienced world works, due to its complexity and our own biased viewpoints and experiences. Writing history, then, depends on the skills, insights and prejudices of its practitioners, who are products of the social, political and historical circumstances in which they live. It is by recognizing this, and examining the implications, that we can hope to reach a closer understanding of earlier peoples, such as the many Iron Age cultures of Europe.

The views of the past which historians and archaeologists produce, then, are coloured by the imperatives of their own present. This is equally true of the ways in which wider society then appropriates and uses these written histories. To take an example related to the case explored in this book, French schoolchildren learn about *nos ancêtres les Gaulois*, 'our ancestors the [Ancient Celtic] Gauls', a link expressed in popular culture through the adventures of the cartoon hero Astérix. But school histories are often as much about promoting modern political ideology as about honestly seeking to understand the past. The identification of modern France with the Ancient Gauls, that romantic, eloquent, fierce, warrior people of Graeco-Roman literature, has long been part of French national mythology. The emperor Napoleon III's excavations at Alesia, scene of the Gauls' last stand against Julius Caesar, and François Mitterrand's sponsorship of the recent major project at the ancient Gallic capital of Mont Beuvray are graphic illustrations of the political significance of the Iron Age in France. It is no less significant in the culture and politics of these islands.

DECONSTRUCTING THE TRADITIONAL
HISTORY OF THE INSULAR CELTS

As we have seen, 'Celtic' is a genuine term in the context of ancient continental Europe, although its exact meaning, and the geographical extent of the Celts, are disputed. In Ireland and Britain the term is an entirely modern usage, whether of living people or their remote ancestors. This means that the story of the insular Celts is not a folk tradition surviving from Antiquity (although certain 'reused' *components* demonstrably are, such as the name Arthur); it was created in remarkably recent times. So, was it a rediscovery of forgotten historical truths, or an invention? If the latter, *why* was it invented? In my view, as will be discussed in chapter 3, the 'canonical' story of the island Celts is much more an invention than a discovery, and the motivations for its creation are to be found not in the Iron Age, but in the political and cultural conflicts of eighteenth-century Europe.

According to the standard versions of the story, the Atlantic Celts remain today the last vestige of a once-great Celtic world originally centred north of the Alps, which especially during the fifth to third centuries BC invaded and colonized in all directions, including the Atlantic islands. This reconstruction of history depends on a number of assumptions. As will be examined in more detail in the next chapter, it assumes that:

- a clearly defined people called Celts existed in continental Europe in the sixth and fifth centuries BC
- we can today define the nature of the Ancient Celts (in terms of specific characteristics of language, religion, art and other material culture, social structure, etc.)
- even though no historical source mentions it, we can use this knowledge to infer the colonization of Britain and Ireland by migrating or invading Celts during the Iron Age. Specifically, this inference depends on demonstrable linguistic affiliations still evident today, and on the more direct testimony of archaeological remains from the Iron Age itself
- there was a fundamental discontinuity with the societies of the preceding New Stone Age and Bronze Age in Britain and Ireland (the age of Newgrange and Stonehenge); the earlier peoples were somehow displaced, whether by expulsion, slaughter or assimilation; often they are not discussed at all, but just 'vanish'
- these immigrant Ancient Celts, regarded as the direct ancestors of the modern insular Celtic peoples, were essentially the same as their modern descendants, who preserve an unchanging 'Celtic spirit'.

In recent years, such 'Celticist' histories, and the assumptions on which they rely, have come under attack from a variety of sources, especially from archaeologists in Britain. Why should this be, especially since the efforts of earlier generations of archaeologists provided some of the larger foundation stones in the Celtic historical edifice? Archaeology identified the art, weapons and other material evidence used to place early Celts in Britain and Ireland. It also seemed to provide material evidence for invasions and migrations from the continent. These were identified through similarities with remains being found on the continent in the nineteenth century, which were themselves being ascribed to the Celtic Gauls – weapons and other artefacts decorated in the remarkable, largely abstract styles which were soon labelled 'Celtic art'. Early insular finds, such as the Waterloo helmet and Battersea shield (see front cover), conveyed a martial aspect which was emphasized when it was established that the great earthwork hillforts of Britain belonged to the same era. The evidence fitted with the aggressive reputation of the continental Celts, and it seemed obvious that the presence of these similarities was due to invasions. After all, Caesar mentioned such incursions, and in a classically educated world, his words carried weight. The Gaulish-style cemetery excavated at Aylesford, Kent, in the 1880s seemed to confirm the idea. However, as will be seen, Caesar's words were used selectively, for migrations or invasions were *expected*; the evidence seemed to confirm a long-established assumption that Celts had arrived in this manner, and so other possible explanations were little considered.

The 'invasion hypothesis' prevailed far into the twentieth century, and the growing body of archaeological evidence continued to be interpreted in terms of it. It all still seemed to fit well when in the 1930s Christopher Hawkes drew up his three-phase 'ABC' scheme to describe the archaeology of the entire British Iron Age and explain it in terms of successive waves of continental Celtic invaders.

But these archaeological interpretations are now discredited, with serious implications for the rest of the Celtic construct. In British archaeology, particularly, major new discoveries after the Second World War threw the whole invasion model of the insular Iron Age into serious doubt. More generally, the last few decades have seen a collapse in long-established theories and assumptions about how human groups develop, function and change. The idea that change in early landscapes is best explained by waves of invaders has been completely discredited. The general background to this revolution is discussed in the next chapter, but evidence specific to the isles is presented here.

Since 1945 there has been an explosion of knowledge about the Iron

Age in the islands, brought about by a huge increase in research effort. The new evidence is also much broader in kind, due to advances in methods and technology, and not least in thinking on what archaeological evidence can tell us. Most notably, to add to the relatively exotic but sparse remains of fine art objects, the spectacular graves of a few rich people, and a limited number of great hillforts, we have now 'found' the great mass of rural populations of the Iron Age (at least in Britain; they remain infuriatingly elusive in Ireland). The evidence for their lives is in the form of many thousands of rural settlements (farmsteads, hamlets, villages) and systems of land division, located by aerial photography, surface survey and excavation. The vastly increased and far more diverse data now available show a very different Iron Age – one which does not fit at all well with the established model.

CONTINUITY WITH CONTACT,
NOT MASS MIGRATION

Had the insular Iron Age indeed consisted of waves of invaders, by now we should have found rich evidence of the kinds of remains characteristic of the supposed Celtic homelands in France and Germany. Not only should there be plenty of identical, or near-identical art and artefacts, but we should also see extensive signs of wholesale transfers of farming regimes and of beliefs and social practices, such as imported burial rites (like the 'flat cemeteries' common in the 'homelands') and, we might surely expect, rectangular continental house types. Such 'intrusive' cultural traces have indeed been found in other areas which historical texts report were colonized by Celts. The Po Valley of northern Italy, where Gallic colonization was recorded in the fifth and fourth centuries BC, has produced important cemeteries which are clearly alien; they represent burial rites completely foreign to earlier local traditions, but which closely parallel those in the postulated areas of origin beyond the Alps. The particular artefacts within, not least decorated metalwork, are often identical to those found beyond the Alps, or very nearly so. These may, according to standard ideas, reasonably be identified as traces of the Gallic invaders and settlers of the histories, some of whom sacked Rome itself around 390 BC.

However, in Britain, and indeed in Ireland, we have found almost none of these predicted traits. To be sure, there are many powerful resonances, in the artistic styles of the Middle and later Iron Age, and in the types of artefacts on which they are found (swords, fittings from wheeled vehicles, types of jewellery). Yet they are far from being the *same*: actual imports are rare, and the examples we have are clearly distinctive insular versions – reinterpretations of continental fashions (figs 6–8). There is also clear evidence for continental *influence* in burial rites, notably in the square-ditched burial mounds of East Yorkshire (a handful of which contain chariots), but such cases are highly localized. Across most of the archipelago, people did not bury the dead at all, but disposed of them in ways leaving no trace. Interestingly, while the Yorkshire burials are clearly connected with similar funerary practices in parts of Gaul, the details of burial are very different (the body is curled up in the 'foetal position' in Yorkshire, but stretched out in Gaul), and the Yorkshire burial goods are local in style, not imports. It seems to have been the *idea* of such burials

6. *The engraved back of a copper alloy mirror from Holcombe, Devon, a classic example of insular La Tène ('Celtic') art dating from the first century* AD. *Such mirrors were a southern British regional speciality.*

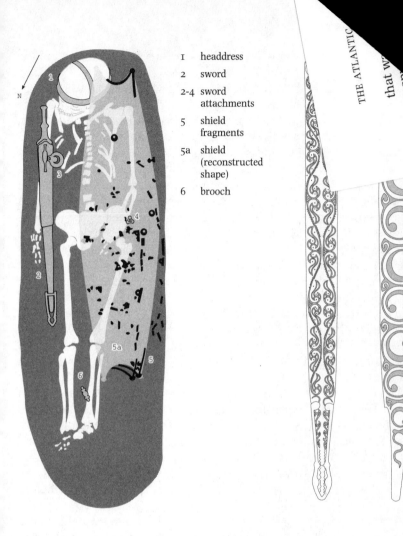

1   headdress

2   sword

2-4 sword
     attachments

5   shield
     fragments

5a   shield
     (reconstructed
     shape)

6   brooch

7. *Warrior burial from Mill Hill, Deal, Kent (c. 200 BC). The warrior's sword and shield are similar to continental Celtic weapons, but distinctly British variants – especially the shape of the shield, with its characteristic concave ends: continental shields had rounded ends.*

8. *Irish sword-scabbard plates in copper alloy decorated with La Tène ornament, from Lisnacrogher, Co. Antrim. Closely related to contemporary British examples, these pieces nevertheless represent a distinctly Irish style. Third century BC.*

...s imported (perhaps as part of a religious belief system), not the
...ulation practising it.

There is no doubt, then, that people in Ireland and Britain were indeed
in contact, often intimate, with people in Gaul. There is thus no reason to
doubt that individuals, and perhaps sometimes small communities,
crossed the Channel, in both directions. But there are no traces of wholesale migrations. On the contrary, the major message of the archaeology
of the Iron Age is not one of continental connection, but of *local continuity
from the preceding Bronze Age*. The major characteristics of British Iron
Age archaeology – for example, circular or ovoid houses, domestic pottery
traditions, farming regimes, and the 'disappearing dead' – are patterns
which were laid down during the local Late Bronze Age, long before the
supposed Iron Age Celtic invasions. The peoples of Iron Age Britain
were not newcomers, but generally seem to have been descendants of
earlier local populations, and similar patterns are observed in Ireland.
And indeed Julius Caesar recorded that British groups considered
themselves to be indigenous. The 'Belgic settlers' from northern Gaul he
mentions continue to be elusive; indeed, the cremation graves which were
taken to be archaeological confirmation of these invaders are now known
to date largely after Caesar's time, and so do not simply represent them
after all.

Mass Celtic migration into Britain is now implausible. Archaeology in
Ireland does not fit with the idea of invasions, either. Barry Raftery, faced
with the consequences of this conclusion, has written, 'It seems almost
heretical to insist that a Celtic invasion of Ireland never happened', and
draws back from the brink, although he concludes enigmatically with a
quote from Tolkien: 'Anything is possible in the fabulous Celtic twilight,
which is not so much a twilight of the gods as of the reason' (Raftery
1994, p. 228).

More generally, as we shall see, we now also have a more sophisticated
understanding of how such 'pre-modern' societies work, largely from
anthropological research on living peoples which shows that they can
and do change, often radically and quickly, for internal reasons as well as
due to external contacts. We do not need to infer invasions to explain the
appearance of similarities between the peoples of Ireland and Britain and
the continental Celtic Gauls (see chapters 4 and 5).

THE GREAT DIVERSITY OF THE ISLANDERS

The other characteristic suggested by the archaeological evidence is the sheer *diversity* of Iron Age communities in the isles. The traditional, popular Iron Age Celtic model implies that all such societies, in places such as Britain, should have been 'essentially' the same, because they all derived from one, homogeneous cultural origin: we therefore expect similar social organization, with a hierarchy of distinct classes or special groups such as warriors, bards and Druids; common religious, military and political ideologies, and typical 'Celtic' material culture – not least La Tène art.

However, the impression given by the overall patterns of archaeological evidence is one of *non*-uniformity. Very few traits indeed are found to be common across the whole of Britain or Ireland. Domestic buildings tend to be round (as we have seen, a Bronze Age trait), but within this they show great regional variation. Even where there are suitable hills, hillforts are far from ubiquitous. Some areas at some periods have major 'central places'; others lack them. Lack of archaeologically detectable burial rites is common, but not universal. The evidence for daily life is also highly varied; for example, pottery was relatively little used in the upland regions. Many areas show little or no sign of the finery of 'Celtic art' or other prestigious artefacts of privileged classes. As will be explored in chapter 5, many of these archaeological patterns are difficult to reconcile with societies organized according to the 'standard' Celtic model with its élite of warriors, nobles, priests and specialized craftsmen.

As a result, the presumption of underlying social uniformity is very much in question. Iron Age variation and diversity need not be seen as 'epiphenomena' – divergences of secondary importance from a 'real' universal norm – but may be the true underlying 'reality'. The archaeological evidence may be interpreted as meaning that there was *no* universal social or cultural norm, but, rather, many different local cultural formations which, to varying degrees, shared and exchanged traits and perhaps in time increasingly converged in certain aspects – just as the societies of medieval and modern Europe have done, while always retaining their different, multiple local cultures and identities.

The early peoples of the archipelago, then, were overwhelmingly of local Bronze Age origin, not invaders from the continental homeland of the 'real' Celts in Gaul. They were actually very diverse, and the physical remains of many communities do not correspond with the standard model of a 'Celtic' society. We cannot even discern a distinctive common

'Britishness' or 'Irishness'; rather, some groups in each island were in contact with, and influencing, each other while, especially in the later Iron Age, some southern and eastern British groups were sharing more and more in common with the Gauls. The evidence suggests that the Iron Age British Isles were not lands of essentially uniform 'Celts', but that both islands were home to complex patterns of multiple identities – as they apparently were in the preceding Bronze Age and certainly have been ever since. If the whole idea of Celts in the islands, and their arrival by migration and invasion from the continent, is a modern construct not supported by archaeological evidence, how and why was it created?

3 How the Celts were Created, and Why

What is the nature of group identities such as the 'Celts'? Of what do they consist, and how are they constructed? This chapter and the next will review the specific case of the Celts against the background of changing general conceptions of peoples and identities, and how they have been defined in recent centuries, from ideas of nation and race to the current concept of ethnicity drawn from the social sciences. It will look at how people have defined group affiliations in their own day, and how they have sought to track earlier ones in history. The main lesson of modern research is that ethnic identities are far less sharply defined and far more complex in structure than is usually assumed, and no easy equations can be made between ethnic names, genetics, language, or material culture. The implications for the reality of the Ancient Celts of the isles are profound.

The key to unravelling the paradox of the Celts is to follow the story of their creation, in the context of contemporary thinking. It is essential to look at the prevailing theoretical understandings of human life at the times when notions of the Celts were being formulated, and indeed in our own time. Thus far in this book I have used terms such as 'people', 'society', 'nation', 'ethnic group', without any very precise definition; but, as will be seen, these are not 'natural' categories, but specific concepts which depend on a particular range of theoretical assumptions about the workings of the world.

'Theory' is a much despised and misunderstood word, often taken to mean 'unproven interpretation', or, further, 'mad idea of misguided person'. A more respectful usage is usually as a contrast to 'fact'; in a common misunderstanding of scientific method (which is still connived at by some scholars), it is assumed that objective facts are collected by dispassionate observers, and theories devised from them. This is profoundly wrong. The very definition of what constitutes facts to be observed and recorded depends on theoretical assumptions. 'Theory' is not something which can be kept in a box until it is needed to apply to some facts; it is inescapably entwined with the decision that certain facts are needed, and the definition of what 'facts' are. In reality, we apply bodies of theory all the time, in everything we say or do; but this is almost entirely unconscious. We hold assumptions about how human societies and history work which are so familiar that we no longer notice them (any more than you notice your own nose, unless you look). All theoretical orientations also always relate to wider cultural trends and political attitudes. We encounter this on the news-stands every day. Patterns of ideologically related assumptions about what constitutes 'facts', and which facts are significant and what they mean, are to be seen in national newspapers, for example in attitudes to the causes of crime and the efficacy of different kinds of punishment. Of course 'ideological bias' is obvious in the papers which do *not* reflect our own views!

To assess any argument, then, it is necessary to consider the terms within which it is framed. Thus, to understand ideas about the Celts, it is essential to look at the cultural and historical contexts which produced them, and to examine the patterns of assumptions and motivations (unconscious, deliberately concealed, or overt) of the people developing them.

THE FIRST APPEARANCE OF INSULAR 'CELTICNESS'

As we have seen, continental peoples called Celts were known in Antiquity, and since the Renaissance the French in particular have placed emphasis on their Celtic Gaulish ancestry. Although as early as 1582 the eminent Scottish scholar George Buchanan proposed that the early Britons were descended from the Gauls, and that Scots Gaelic was also derived from Gaulish, the notion of *insular* Celts and Celticness finds its genesis as late as the first years of the eighteenth century. It was launched in the writings of the great Welsh scholar and patriot Edward Lhuyd (or Lhwyd; he spelt his name more than one way). Lhuyd, who became Keeper of the Ashmolean Museum in Oxford, had undertaken years of dogged fieldwork and research into the grammatical structures and vocabularies of the languages, ancient and modern, of Ireland, Scotland, Wales, Cornwall and Brittany. He was also spurred on by the writings of his Breton contemporary Paul-Yves Pezron, whose *Antiquité de la nation, et de langue des Celtes, autrement appellez Gaulois* (1703) suggested that modern Welsh and Breton were survivals of the ancient language of the continental Gauls, or Celts (although he does not directly speak of either contemporary 'Celtic' language or people, in Britain or Brittany, in the original French edition). Pezron's book sets out an elaborate genealogy of the continental Celts and their language involving complex migrations. The idea of the migration of Gaulish/Celtic speakers (= Gauls/Celts) into Britain is implicit. However, Pezron was not especially interested in Britain, and said nothing of Ireland; his purpose was more to establish the historical pedigree of the Bretons in continental Europe, and especially as a people separate from the French. For the Bretons stood in much the same relation to France as the Welsh and others stood to England, i.e. a self-aware people who faced reduction to the status of peripheral province of a large homogenizing nation-state. Pezron was helping to establish their antiquity and cultural separateness from France, as Lhuyd was doing vis-à-vis England.

In the Bodleian library, Oxford, I have examined Lhuyd's own inscribed copy of Pezron's work, which electrified him. I got a considerable frisson myself out of handling this physical evidence of the intellectual interaction of Pezron and Lhuyd (who never actually met), a volume which is, in a way, the primary material relic of the creation of the insular Celts. Lhuyd was apparently instrumental in arranging for rapid Welsh and English translations of Pezron's book. The latter, published in 1706, has a significant addition to the title: *The Antiquities of Nations, More particularly of the Celtae or Gauls, Taken to be Originally the same People as our Ancient Britains* [sic].

Lhuyd published his own contribution in 1707. His *Archaeologia Britannica* was intended as the first volume of a larger work which would also deal with monuments, although he did not live to produce the rest. The book was a significant landmark in the history of the study of language (today subdivided into contemporary linguistics and the more historically orientated philology). It demonstrated the underlying similarities of what he saw as a family of recent and current languages, which he also showed were related to the extinct language of the Ancient Gauls of France. Although not entirely explicit on the subject, in this book he attached the name 'Celtic' to this family of tongues. In the book, his usage of the term is not very consistent, but the section 'A Comparative Vocabulary of the Original Languages of Britain and Ireland' is also referred to in the Preface as a 'sort of Latin-Celtic Dictionary', or a 'Latin-Celtic or Comparative Vocabulary'. By implication, then, the original languages of Britain and Ireland were Celtic tongues. Lhuyd also used the term of contemporary insular languages, writing of '. . . the Celtique, which is spoken in Wales, Cornwall [*sic*] and Bass Bretagne [*sic*; i.e. Brittany].'

Subsequently, Lhuyd's Celtic family was refined, and two distinct branches recognized, referred to as 'Goidelic' or 'Q-Celtic' (Irish and Scots Gaelic, and Manx), and 'Brythonic' or 'P-Celtic' (Welsh, Cornish and Breton) (fig. 9).

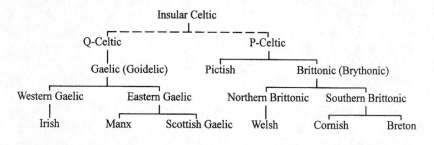

9. One current view of the relationships between the modern Celtic languages (after Macauley 1992).

But why did Lhuyd choose the name 'Celtic' at all? So far as I can tell, no direct evidence survives regarding his motivation. Perhaps the family was simply named after the earliest attested member of the group, the language of the Ancient Gauls: he could hardly have called it the 'Gallic' family, since the term was identified with France, the perennial enemy, but according to the venerated writings of Julius Caesar most of the Gauls were called *Celtae*, and 'Celtic' was not politically compromised.

In the Welsh preface to his own book, Lhuyd outlined an idea of how these languages came to be established in Britain and Ireland, through a scheme of prehistoric migration of people from Gaul to occupy the whole of Britain, whence some of them moved on to become, with Scots originally from Spain, the Irish. While he clearly envisioned all these migrant peoples speaking languages of his 'Celtic' family, he did not call them 'Celts'. Nevertheless, here is the basis for the subsequently popular idea of the islands being taken over by waves of Ancient Celts.

Once Lhuyd had launched the idea of Celtic-*speakers*, ancient and modern, in the isles, the label was quickly used also to describe cultural or national *identities*, past and present; and both ideas became accepted as established fact throughout Britain and Ireland with remarkable speed. By 1723, Lhuyd's friend and fellow-countryman Henry Rowlands was writing of 'We the Celtae . . .'. The following year the great antiquarian William Stukeley was using the word 'Celtic' of ancient monuments in the British landscape – it was already becoming a term used to describe material remains. Over the following decades, educated society at large incorporated the Celts into their understanding of the history of the isles: by 1773 Johnson and Boswell could encounter a clergyman in the Hebrides who believed there had been Ancient Celts from Asia Minor to Skye. By 1817 Sir Walter Scott could refer in a novel to eighteenth-century Scottish Highlanders as Celts, without feeling any need to elaborate (*Rob Roy*, chapters XXII and XXIII). In just a century the Celts became established popular fact, the circumstances and recent date of their appearance generally forgotten.

But *why* was the idea of insular Celticness and 'people called Celts' so extraordinarily successful in the eighteenth century? Was it because it revealed an ancient, but hitherto hidden, historical reality? Or does the answer lie in the eighteenth century itself? For me, the evidence is unambiguous. On the one hand, there is no doubt that the insights into language made by Pezron and Lhuyd were perfectly real, and Lhuyd's work in particular is justly celebrated as a great scholarly achievement. However, it was also remarkably timely, in providing the basis for a wholly new conception of the identities and histories of the non-English peoples of the isles, which at that moment were under strong political and cultural threat. The idea of being Celts, with a deep indigenous ancestry, fulfilled a pressing need.

It is, at the very least, a remarkably fortuitous coincidence that the concept of Celtic speakers, and by implication ethnic Celts, in Britain, Brittany and Ireland was first published in 1707. That was the very year that the Treaty of Union between England and Scotland saw the official creation of a new *political* identity called 'British'. The Union was largely a measure by the English/Welsh and Scottish Protestant establishments to forestall two linked threats facing them at the time: the power of France and the perceived dangers of Catholicism, which was soon to manifest itself in the Jacobite risings in Scotland. The recurrent military threat from France, a major driving force in British overseas empire-building, climaxed again with the French Revolutionary and Napoleonic Wars, which precipitated the forcible extension of the Union to incorporate

Ireland into the United Kingdom through the Act of 1800. The course of the eighteenth century saw an attempt to deepen the political union by creating a new sense of joint British national identity, which inevitably was dominated by the most powerful partner, England: still today Europeans and Americans – and too often the English themselves – say 'English' where they mean 'British' as a whole. Non-English identities faced potential cultural oblivion through assimilation and submergence into a common Britishness which was overwhelmingly English in character.

With the signing of the 1707 Treaty, then, the name of Briton – the best, and time-honoured, potential collective label for those peoples of the island who saw themselves as other than English – was appropriated for all subjects of the new, inevitably English-dominated superstate. (Lhuyd himself used 'Britons' and 'British' as synonyms for 'Welsh people' and 'Welsh language', expressing their historical descent from, and continuity with, the Ancient Britons, a usage which the new state terminology rendered confusing.) At that same moment Lhuyd provided the 'terminologically dispossessed' groups with a new collective name and identity: 'Celtic'. I believe that the state usurpation of the name 'Briton' was a key reason for the success and speed of uptake of the label 'Celtic' during the eighteenth century and its subsequent establishment in popular culture. It also had the key advantage of including that other people whose identity was under threat, the Irish, which 'British' never had.

As the nineteenth century approached, the notion of insular 'Celticness' touched a range of other nerves too, and even non-Celtic speakers, the English and Lowland Scots, found reasons, positive and negative, to accept it. A major reason for the popularity of the Celts and everything associated with the idea was a profound shift in perception of Highland Scotland, both the landscape and the people who dwelt there. This was brought about by two linked processes. The destruction of Highland society in the generations following the slaughter at Culloden in 1746 meant that the Highlanders were no longer perceived as an actual menace to 'civilized' life. At the same time, the growing self-confidence of the rising industrial classes was establishing the general belief in progress, and the power of humanity to achieve whatever it liked, that characterized the expansionist nineteenth century. This made the landscapes of areas like the Highlands no longer seem so threatening or desolate. It became possible to romanticize both the vanishing culture and the countryside, which was now deemed wildly beautiful. This constituted an immensely attractive romantic Other, to contrast with the regimented drabness of factory and city which was the lot of increasing numbers of people – not least exiles from the glens, and their children who had never lived there. Those who were driven or drawn overseas from Scotland, Ireland or Wales similarly looked back on a nostalgic past, set in aspic. The Highland Scottish element, at least, was largely the creation of one man, Sir Walter Scott, whose Waverley novels disseminated the idea of the noble clansman: his efforts culminated in triumph when the Hanoverian George IV visited Scotland and wore a kilt in 1822. This royal sanction for what, fifty years before, had been a despised and illegal mode of dress of dangerous peripheral 'barbarians' led to the craze for Highland garb and allegedly ancient clan tartans which has persisted ever since.

The hunger for this romantic Celtic antiquity is also seen in the enormous Europe-wide popularity of the poems of 'Ossian'. Allegedly the works of an early Highland bard 'discovered' by James MacPherson in 1760 but actually modern pastiches, they nevertheless whetted the appetite for rediscovering the genuine treasures of early literature in Celtic languages. Another product of the period was the obsession with Druidism, which had been launched by William Stukeley.

There was also a darker side to the enthusiasm for Celtic distinctiveness, which came more to the fore in the nineteenth century: racial, as well as cultural distinction came to be made between Celts and Anglo-Saxons. This could be to the political advantage of the former, as it might give them the prestige of being a distinct population with prior claim to the islands; however, it was fashionable among (largely Anglo-Saxon) scientists, and useful to many politicians, to rank racial groups, with (inevitably) whites at the top and blacks at the bottom. Celts – especially the Irish – were widely deemed to be whites inferior to Anglo-Saxons. This helped to give a scientific gloss to discrimination, in a world where poorer Anglo-Saxons were also considered inferior, and in which Malthusian beliefs about population, later to develop into Social Darwinism and eugenics, established the mindset which could allow disasters like the Irish potato famine (and indeed starvation in the English countryside) to pass with little attempt at relief.

During the eighteenth and nineteenth centuries, then, societies throughout the isles had a variety of reasons to take up the new notion of Celticness with enthusiasm. However, I believe that Lhuyd was not simply a scholar who fortuitously came up with the right idea at the right time: to a large extent, he knew what he was doing, and had a political agenda clearly in mind.

Lhuyd's forerunners and contemporaries at Oxford and elsewhere had been studying early documents and the language in which they were written to build up a picture of the early English, not least for political reasons: to give English identity a good historical pedigree. As a Welsh patriot as well as a talented linguistic scholar, Lhuyd sought to do the same for his own country, and for its non-English neighbours, who also shared an uncomfortable bed with the English elephant. They, like the Welsh, often suffered at the hands of English political power, prejudice and cultural and religious arrogance. Lhuyd's work was instrumental in providing the non-English peoples with an academically authoritative, shared historical pedigree far deeper than their individual national histories, and older by a thousand years than that of the English. How far he was *consciously* attempting to achieve this is not certain, but his surviving correspondence suggests that he had a pretty good idea of the implications of his work. In a postscript to a letter he penned on Michaelmas Day 1703 to the Revd John Lloyd of Ruthin, Denbighshire, Lhuyd wrote:

One Abbot PEZRON, an Armorique Britan [sic: i.e., a Breton], has lately published his *Antiquité de la Nation et de la langue Gauloise*; wherein he has infinitely outdone all our Countreymen [sic; i.e., the Welsh] *as to national zeal* [my italics]. He proves that they and we are the onely [sic] nations in the world that have the honour to have preserv'd the language of Jupiter and Sadurn [sic], whom he shews to have been Princes of the Titans, the progenitors of the Gauls . . .'

(Gunther 1945, pp. 489-90, Letter 247)

While he was writing his *magnum opus*, then, Lhuyd was thinking very much in terms of competing modern national identities, and their legitimation through their ancient connections and pedigrees.

This passage also shows the – to us – strange ideas of the seventeenth and eighteenth centuries about the nature of peoples and their origins. Pezron had followed the common practice, established in the sixteenth century, of tracing the genealogy of European nations, peoples and languages back to a complex web of roots in both biblical and classical mythology and history, connecting them to the established and dominant Judaeo-Christian religious tradition and to the prestigious Graeco-Roman world. The following selection of chapter titles outlines part of the convoluted genealogy of the Celts and their language, as envisioned by Pezron:

BOOK I

Such speculations on the origins of peoples look bizarre to us today: no one would now accept, for instance, anything as preposterous as Celtic origins for the Spartans, let alone the descent of the Celts from figures in classical myth. However, they were established, indeed perfectly respectable features of academic discourse on national origins at the time. This also makes the point that the 'traditional' views held today of the origins of the Celts in late prehistoric Central Europe were not yet developed in the time of Pezron and Lhuyd: they were to depend on new discoveries, on the development of new disciplines, and also on radical changes in philosophy and theory, not least the development of fully secular scholarship during the nineteenth century. Lhuyd was so influential in the eighteenth century not least because philology (the study of languages, especially through historical and comparative approaches) carried great prestige, at a time before the development of those other disciplines which today study past and present human societies. To be sure, early antiquarians and ethnographers were already producing important and fascinating work, but anthropology, sociology and archaeology appeared as disciplines only in the nineteenth century.

Since the Renaissance, the story of Western ideas about the nature and interrelationships of human groups reveals that the very terms and categories we have used to describe them – 'peoples', 'races', 'societies', 'tribes', 'nations' and, most recently, 'ethnicities' – are not natural and inevitable ones: they are themselves the products of our own peculiar Western traditions, assumptions and prejudices about the world. These ideas, as one can see in Pezron's work on the Celts quoted above, are ultimately based on earlier biblical and Graeco-Roman traditions. For example, the notion that peoples share a family tree derives largely from the belief in common descent from Noah, whose children gave rise to the various nations of the world; hence the Semites are sons of Shem, etc. Such eponymous ancestors led to the idea that the named peoples involved are kin-related, sharing the same 'blood', and are likely to be thought of as distinctly bounded, homogeneous entities.

The surviving classical accounts, not least of the 'barbarians' of Northern Europe, incorporate similar ideas about peoples, and these, too, have influenced the recent Western tradition. Greece passed on to the Romans its view of the shape of the world, which, like that of other civilizations, saw itself as the ordered centre of the universe, while others were seen as peripheral, strange and inferior; the further away, the more bizarre and literally outlandish they were assumed to be. Their particular cosmological beliefs and expectations, of a quite geometric arrangement of 'barbarian' groups around the periphery, meant that they tended to see all the 'barbarians' of each of the four cardinal points as much the same: Scythians in the north, Persians in the east, Libyans in the south, and Celts in the west. Thus, they perceived and represented the continental Gauls in a certain way, which was only partially modified by direct experience and observation. Given these cosmological prejudices, it is unsurprising that Graeco-Roman writers regarded the peoples of Britain and Ireland as weird in a degree appropriate to groups actually living in the midst of *Oceanus*, the dreaded, monster-filled seas at the edge of the world, and duly focused on tales of inverted gender roles in Britain and of cannibalism among the Irish. However, they did not regard the peoples of the islands as the same as the Gauls (although they were aware of important similarities and contacts), and crucially, as we have seen, no ancient source ever calls insular people 'Celts'. Indeed, Strabo contrasts Britons and Celts. Caesar, who provides us with the first clear eyewitness account from his large-scale raids of 55 and 54 BC, noted the similarities of the coastal districts with Gaul, and recorded a tradition of some recent Gallic settlement. In the first century AD, Tacitus speculated on connections of western British groups with peoples in Hispania. By contrast, Caesar records that the peoples of the interior of Britain believed themselves to be indigenous to the island, a view repeated by the Greek Diodorus Siculus.

Neither did they regard the peoples of Britain as homogeneous. When the Romans annexed the south of Britain and tried to conquer the north, they continued to record perceived local distinctions, mentioning the various *civitates* (a term which originally referred to the city-states characteristic of Rome's own Mediterranean world, but given a more general meaning of 'self-governing community' like the English word 'polity'; its usual modern translation in the context of Britain as 'tribes' says more about recent views of these entities than about the Romans' ideas). More generally, they also distinguished between *Britanni* in the south and *Brittones* in the north (although we do not know what the distinction was, or whether this was a wholly Roman division, or reflected local people's own self-categorizations).

These biblical and Graeco-Roman ideas and observations formed the basis of scholarly thinking when ideas about insular Celts were being formulated in the eighteenth and nineteenth centuries. Scholars tended to think in terms of neatly bounded, named 'peoples' or 'nations'. We may be inherently inclined to think along such lines: the human mind, and language, tend to work in terms of fairly simple and vivid symbols. In the teeming complexity of the world, we seek patterns which are simple enough to hold in our minds and to express briefly in words; inevitably, these shorthand expressions are often oversimplified. In the case of group identities, we may see 'Us', and especially the various groups of 'Them', in very stereotypical terms.

Contemporary 'peoples' and 'nations' considered in the abstract, then, are still commonly conceived as being clearly *bounded* and *homogeneous*, their constituent individuals sharing clear, uniform cultural characteristics. This view tends to downplay the importance of, or even render invisible, any significant variation within these units, and ignores the possibility that societies may grade imperceptibly into each other. Today, this is encouraged by the notion of nation-states within which we live, but which are themselves a recent innovation, very different from earlier social organizations. Take the example of 'the French': you can tell, to the inch, where France ends; whether someone is a French citizen from their papers; the French language is *par excellence* a feature of Frenchness; there is characteristic French 'material culture' – food, drink, clothing, architecture, etc. But these rather stereotypical images are still retained even when one knows, and has perhaps seen, the differences between the distinctive peoples of Brittany, Provence, Corsica, Alsace or multi-cultural Paris or Lyon. The people of Quebec are not part of France, but consider themselves French, with another distinctive culture. French identity is not as clearly bounded, and nowhere near as homogeneous, as we tend to think.

We tend to see the past, too, as consisting of neatly bounded identity groups (city-states, tribes, etc.) which echo the supposed sharp edges of our own familiar nation-states. But since such images are actually poor descriptions even of modern nations, we should not assume that 'peoples' in the past were necessarily any more clearly defined.

From the early nineteenth century, in a development closely linked with the rise of romantic nationalisms in Europe, scholars became very interested in the distinctions between human groups, how these are manifested and how they may be characterized. The main concept used throughout the nineteenth century was that of 'race', although there was much disagreement about exactly what this meant, especially before the development of modern biology and the science of genetics. While some placed emphasis on comparative anatomy in an attempt to trace actual biological distinctions between populations, others placed much greater weight on similarities of language as evidence for identity. This cultural approach derived from the great prestige of philological studies, and also from ethnological studies of living peoples in other parts of the world (which led to the development of modern anthropology during the nineteenth century). The thinking behind this tradition, and many specific early ideas about patterns of common ancestry, derived from the biblical tradition which lay at the root of European scholarship.

The issue of race was relevant not only to the emotionally charged issue of the relations of whites, deemed inherently superior to all others (if indeed they were related at all; some argued for separate 'creations'). Racial distinction was also an issue among whites, of a presumed hierarchy of 'superiority' of peoples and nations. Most relevantly, the 'Anglo-Saxon' Protestant élite in the British Isles and North America looked down on allegedly lesser European 'racial' groups, who were thought to be less industrious and upright: such groups included Slavs, Jews and southern Europeans such as Italians. It was assumed that such 'racial characteristics' were ingrained from antiquity.

Whatever the particular emphasis, 'race' was used generally and often very loosely throughout the nineteenth century as a synonym for national, cultural and linguistic groups, which were assumed to be essentially coincident in extent. There was an assumption and expectation that peoples, whether 'primitive' or 'civilized', could be clearly defined and were essentially homogeneous. After all, as we have seen, this was – and is – how many Westerners envisioned the nation-states of which they were citizens at the time.

It was also tacitly assumed that 'primitive' societies were fundamentally static and unchanging. Later, assumptions of 'primitive timelessness' about human cultures would be shown to be simply wrong: they were based on arrogant assumptions of the superiority and progress of 'Anglo-Saxon' industrial imperialism. But while they prevailed, they had major implications for how changes visible in the record of the past were to be explained. If societies did not innovate, then changes – such as new ranges of artefacts, styles of art, types of monument or burial rite – had to be explained by incursions of people from elsewhere, usually interpreted as migration or invasion, bringing upheaval and the probable destruction of the indigenous groups. This presumed fate reflected all too well what was happening to many peoples under the wheels of European colonialism at the time.

The insular Celts, ancient and contemporary, came to be conceptualized in terms of, and in resistance to, these dominant modes of thinking. They came to be portrayed, in a largely negative and often sinister way, as the antithesis of the Anglo-Saxons, contrasting in all respects with the 'masculine' qualities of industry, imperial vigour and progress of the latter. The Celtic peoples, ancient and modern, were characterized as 'timeless' in this way, and widely seen as primitive, even barbaric. The alleged characteristics of the Celtic 'race(s)' were associated with the feminine, and with backwardness and inferiority; the Irish, particularly, were often viciously stereotyped as wild, dissolute, drunken and (probably worst) Catholic. It was easier to demonize them as irredeemably brutal and primitive than to acknowledge the injustices of a colonial regime in Ireland which dispossessed and disenfranchised the majority Catholic population, and was at least partly responsible for conditions which exposed millions to starvation, desperation and exile.

Of course, among the Celtic peoples themselves, very different assessments became prevalent in the nineteenth century, although largely governed by the same set of assumptions about race and the timelessness of ancient traditions. It was a period of major social upheaval throughout the islands, with enormous suffering and major migrations from rural areas, both internally to the industrial cities and overseas. The Irish potato famine and the Highland Clearances in particular all helped to spur nationalist and cultural movements (see chapter 5). Both were, after all, human disasters brought about largely by economic and political (in)action governed by the kind of colonialist ideology discussed above, which made it 'inevitable' that the weak and inferior should suffer. At a time when romantic nationalisms prevailed across Europe, it is unsurprising that those who suffered at home, or who were forced into exile, should also have developed more explicit notions of national and 'racial' identity. During the nineteenth century the theme of Celticness was of great importance in the growing movements towards mass, national self-consciousness in Wales, Scotland and Ireland. The very antiquity implied by being Celts was a source of pride and of cultural self-confidence, with the implicit prior claim to legitimacy in the isles. Much of this was expressed in cultural terms, through for example the 'Celtic revival' in Ireland. To many non-Celts, a positive reading of Celtic Otherness as romantic, ancient, mysterious and wildly exciting (notably the icon of the free-spirited Scottish Highlander) was immensely attractive. But Celtic consciousness also became overtly political, at least in Ireland (see chapter 5).

With the Celts established as a living cultural tradition, there was great interest in their presumed deep history, thought to stretch back far beyond even the distant genesis of the individual, contemporary Celtic nations. This profound antiquity was a key aspect of the very idea of the insular Celts. The assumption that Ancient Celts had existed in Britain and Ireland before the Romans was already taken for granted before any-one had discovered how to identify with confidence traces belonging to the period. Thus, when systematic archaeology developed in Britain, finds were classified and labelled in terms of a predetermined Celtic framework.

Many ancient artefacts and early sites were already known, but neither their relative sequence in history, nor their precise dates had been deter-mined. The idea of deep geological time, rather than the few thousand years given by standard biblical chronologies, was becoming established during the first half of the nineteenth century, giving human history much greater potential depth, too. This was the situation when scientific archaeology arose in the later nineteenth century and made the first inroads into the task of reconstructing the shape and development of pre-historic human life in Europe. The demonstration that stone had given way to bronze and then iron as the (literally) 'cutting edge technology' led to the definition of the 'Three Age System', and by the end of the century the notion of the European Iron Age had become widely accepted and its general conformation was beginning to be mapped out.

During Victorian times, as scientific excavation began to develop, major discoveries in mainland Europe were ascribed, with considerable confidence, to the continental Celts or Gauls of the classical texts. Of par-ticular importance were the finds at Hallstatt in Austria and La Tène in Switzerland. At Hallstatt, many richly furnished Early Iron Age graves were excavated. The finds proved to be related to material from a wide region north of the Alps, and seemed to correspond in time and place to the earliest Greek references to *Keltoi* (around the sixth century BC). Deposits of different kinds of artefacts, probably religious water-offerings, from the bed of Lake Neuchâtel at La Tène, also belonged to a wider pattern of affiliations. The characteristic items found there were related to objects recovered from burials, especially in eastern France and the Rhine basin, which could be dated to the fifth and fourth centuries BC by the imported Greek and Etruscan vessels of well-known and well-dated types buried with them. Again on grounds of date and geographical location, these remains were identified with the Celts or Gauls which classical sources reported had poured into Italy from just these areas around 400 BC. The unique traits of the artefacts, and details of deposition, such as the rites of burial, became identified as characteristic of Celtic Gaulish peoples, and the areas of eastern France and the Rhine basin where they first developed became thought of as the 'Celtic homelands'. They apparently fitted very well with the Graeco-Roman portrait of Gauls, notably the emphasis on weapons of war, wheeled vehicles interpreted as chariots, splendid jewellery, and equipment for drinking and feasting.

This 'package' of archaeological features eventually became known to archaeologists as the 'La Tène culture', after the Swiss 'type-site'. The strange but glorious swirling, largely abstract decoration with which they were covered became technically known as the 'La Tène style', or more colloquially as 'Celtic art'. Because of the ways people thought about material culture, what it meant and how elements of it moved around, these stylistic traits, artefacts and site characteristics were seen as ethnic signifiers: finds of 'La Tène'-type artefacts or traces of rites elsewhere were generally presumed to represent the presence of Celts. Because of these supposed close and neat equations of material culture and a named people, when it was established that La Tène art, especially, found its genesis in the fifth century in eastern France and the Rhine basin and had spread west, it was widely assumed that this neatly reflected Celtic migrations. The alternative possibility – that it was cultural traits, fashions, habits which were being transmitted, not entire 'peoples' moving – was not considered, although such cultural transmissions were the everyday experience of Europe at the time. This was largely because 'primitive' peoples were thought to be incapable of significant 'progress', so that such innovations must mean migrations.

The islands had evidently been too distant to receive the Greek and Etruscan imported objects which were so crucial to the early establishment of Iron Age chronology on the continent; they also generally lacked the kinds of cemeteries rich in artefacts from which much of the early archaeology of Gaul was initially written. But, just as the early Gauls were first identified through the presence of artefacts relating their remains chronologically to those of the well-known classical Mediterranean, so the insular Iron Age was initially approached through identifying similarities with the archaeology of the Gauls. In the mid-nineteenth century two objects which were destined to become icons of the British Iron Age were dredged from the bed of the Thames: the Battersea shield and the 'horned helmet' found at Waterloo Bridge. Both embellished in abstract, curving decoration, their intimate relationship to the Gaulish finds was increasingly apparent, and they would become recognized as major finds of La Tène art. They were lodged in the British Museum, where already in the 1860s A.W. Franks, Keeper of British and Medieval collections, described them as 'late Keltic'. The archaeology of the insular Iron Age, preconceived as Celtic, was beginning to be formulated.

The demonstration that many British hillforts belonged to the Iron Age further seemed to fit well with the received model of warlike Celts. Other early archaeological finds also demonstrated strong connections across the Channel, notably the cremation cemetery at Aylesford, Kent, excavated late in the nineteenth century, which is clearly a part of the same cultural tradition prevailing at the time in Gaul. Surely here were Caesar's Belgic invaders? The evidence through which the archaeology of the Iron Age was first identified seemed to fit with the idea that Britain and Ireland had been culturally much the same as Gaul, and indeed with the idea of 'heroic' societies (as in Gaul, the artefacts in Britain also strongly emphasized war, display and feasting) apparently arriving by invasions from the mainland. However, because the archaeology of the Iron Age had to be identified primarily through the comparative method, it is unsurprising that at first it looked very similar indeed to the remains from Gaul: the very method employed meant that insular Iron Age remains which did not resemble the Gallic equivalents could not be recognized at all! This problem was greatly exacerbated because it took archaeologists decades to establish how to recognize and date the more ephemeral traces of Iron Age life, especially the remains of the largely earth and timber settlements of the mass of the population, which after the Second World War were to reveal a very different Iron Age.

In this way, archaeology became an important, if relatively late, contributor to the creation of the insular Ancient Celts, a process which saw the extension of the meaning of 'Celtic' in the isles from the speakers of a group of related languages to a single named people, sharing one essentially uniform cultural tradition, spanning the whole archipelago and more than 2,000 years of history. The nineteenth century saw the gradual development of a clear, normative view of what 'Ancient Celts' were like. It was already established on linguistic grounds that there were speakers of languages we call Celtic in the early British Isles, and that these might be called 'Celts'; it was assumed on the basis of biblical notions of peoples and their dissemination that their presence was to be explained by migration; a somewhat selective reading of classical texts seemed to support ideas of invasions in later prehistory; and much of the first identified archaeology obviously related to the material identified as belonging to the continental Gauls or Celts – weapons and other fine metalwork, as well as funerary pottery. In the latter part of the nineteenth century, then, archaeology seemed to add a concrete materiality to the Celtic paradigm, a scientific sanction of documented, dated remains, where before there had been speculation about stone circles and burial-mounds (archaeologists now demonstrated that these belonged to pre-Iron Age times). It seems to me that this is a good example of the process of 'reification', the conversion of an abstraction into a thing, an entity which may exist only in the minds of the beholders.

INTO THE TWENTIETH CENTURY:
'RACE' GIVES WAY TO 'CULTURE'

During the later nineteenth century, in an attempt to achieve more accurate and sophisticated descriptions of human societies, and not least with a mind to distancing liberal scholarship from the often sinister uses of racial terminology, anthropologists began to describe contemporary non-Western peoples in terms of distinctive 'cultures'. The notion of multiple cultures in the present caught on, and was soon extended to interpretation of the mute, fragmentary archaeological remains of past human groups as well. It was so successful that, outside physical anthropology, it generally displaced the concept of 'race' in the social sciences during the twentieth century, and to a large extent the change also affected popular usage, especially since the racist excesses of the Nazis.

However, the idea of groups as 'cultures' carried over many presuppositions from the previous three centuries, not least a continuing expectation that human societies can be defined in terms of clear 'boundedness' and essential internal homogeneity. There was a presumption that anthropological 'cultures', which in the present were generally equated with named peoples, would tend to have distinctive languages or dialects, and characteristic ways of life, including social organization, beliefs, rituals and traits of 'material culture', from details of house layout and construction to modes of dress and ways of decorating pottery. These characteristics, which marked out one culture as different from neighbouring cultures, were expected – indeed usually presumed – to share common, well-defined boundaries.

Another established assumption which was carried over into the 'cultural' approach was the essential unchangingness of 'primitive' peoples: the rapid changes actually observed were put down to the impact of the modern imperial West, which was presumed to be characterized by its march to improvement – 'progress' was a key aspect of its superiority over these 'lesser' societies. The impact of Western civilization on indigenous cultures was seen in terms of 'acculturation', their simple and direct adoption of (in this case, Western) culture and habits, leading to their assimilation and the disappearance of indigenous cultural traditions. (Such a view assumed that artefacts and other cultural traits have fixed meanings; if people adopt them, and use them differently, it is because they fail to understand them properly, and so may look incompetent. It does not allow that the recipients may be reinterpreting foreign traits intelligently, in terms of their own cultural values.) Whether the visible alterations of 'native peoples' in contact with Western powers represented beneficial progress or the corruption of their 'pure cultures' was – and still is – a matter of debate. Inherent tendency to change, in the absence of the 'dynamic' West, was still not thought typical. Representation of 'tribes' and 'societies' as abstract static entities each with unchanging 'primitive' culture was commonplace from the 1920s to the 1960s, especially in British anthropology. Discontinuity or heterogeneity were usually considered as fleeting and exceptional abnormalities.

The same set of presumptions was also carried over into archaeology and applied to the case of the Celts among many others. In many ways archaeologists faced an even more difficult task than anthropologists in trying to tease out the social organization of human groups, as their subjects have vanished and are now represented only by fragmentary, decayed and distorted traces of their material world. Sometimes – as in the case of the Iron Age Celts – this was supplemented by equally fragmentary documentary material, further refracted through the presuppositions and prejudices of other, intermediary societies. The idea that patterning within the archaeological record, which could certainly be seen, related directly to 'cultures' as understood by anthropologists, was highly attractive, and seemed to make excellent sense.

For much of the twentieth century archaeological thinking in many parts of the world has been framed in terms of a 'cultural-historical' approach, developed by scholars such as Gustav Kossinna in Germany and V. Gordon Childe in Britain. Kossinna strongly emphasized the supposedly clear equations of archaeological 'cultures' defined through shared traits of characteristic artefacts and practices with specific, named peoples. His work focused on the genealogies of modern peoples, especially the Germans; after his death it was taken up by the Nazis, which resulted in the retrospective tainting of his reputation, while less controversial aspects of his work continued to have strong influence. But in Britain, especially, it was Childe who was the doyen of 'cultural-historical' archaeology. In 1929 he defined an archaeological culture as 'certain types of remains, houses, burial rites, artefacts, constantly occurring together'. Later he saw groups of artefacts as 'common tools which bind together a people': the equation of a 'culture' and its boundaries with a distinct 'people' was usually at least implicitly assumed under this approach. Childe wanted a whole assemblage of artefact types and other cultural traits to define such archaeological cultures, but sometimes a single new pot-type was used to define a new 'culture' and, overtly or by implication, the appearance of a new people.

Not surprisingly, if modern, observable 'primitive' peoples were still presumed to be 'timeless' and unchanging, the same presumption was applied to societies in the past. Observed changes therefore could not be due to internal developments. There were circumstances where early societies were clearly exposed to 'higher' civilizations, and the resulting changes could be explained in terms of acculturation. Rome, as a major model for modern European imperialism, was thought to have related to many 'barbarian' cultures in France and Britain much as white colonialists were believed to relate to peoples in Africa or Asia. The idea of 'Romanization' is essentially acculturation projected into the past: peoples such as the Gauls and southern Britons were believed to have adopted Roman ways wholesale, resulting in the obliteration of their

Celtic culture. In the case of the latter, the resulting Romano-British culture often appeared as a pale, sad, even ludicrously incompetent aping of the civilization of Roman Italy, because the meanings of Roman culture were assumed to be fixed. It was therefore appropriate to judge the apparent success or failure of Romano-British culture against Italian standards, rather than seeing it in its own terms – as the selective adaptation of aspects of Roman ways by societies which had limited use for Italian aristocratic artistic traditions.

But until almost the time of Caesar near the end of the Iron Age, the insular peoples had no such 'higher' cultural neighbour to inspire change. The many innovations increasingly visible in the archaeological record across the islands had to be explained by other means, and, as we have seen, a presumption that mass invasions or migrations were a common feature of human history had long been generally accepted. Since these were regarded as primitive cultures, the successive changes which were also increasingly evident in the data had to be explained by outside agency: changes in burial rites or in pottery design, the introduction of new kinds of weapons, were often explained as the result of the well-established (but little tested) presumed mechanisms of migration and invasion. Such assumptions are evident in the chronological scheme devised by Christopher Hawkes for the British Iron Age in 1931, which came to be known as the 'ABC' scheme, the three phases of which were primarily envisioned as representing waves of invaders from Gaul.

THE LATER TWENTIETH CENTURY:
THE DISCREDITING OF ESTABLISHED
ASSUMPTIONS

. . . the idea of a bounded, monolithic cultural cum ethnic unit is also a modern classificatory myth projected onto all of human history.

(Jones 1997, p. 104)

Since the late 1960s, there has been a revolution in how we think about human groups. It is necessary to outline this in some detail, because it has profound implications for the established view of the existence, and nature, of Ancient Celts in the isles.

Although the idea of 'cultures' remained the dominant approach in anthropology until the 1960s, and the derivative 'culture-historical' method prevailed in archaeology longer still (and remains widespread today), for many decades the inadequacies of such approaches have been increasingly apparent. There is now plentiful evidence that the fundamental assumptions underlying them are quite wrong. Typically, human 'cultures' are not sharply bounded and neither are they usually homogeneous internally. Further, 'primitive' societies are not 'timeless', but dynamic and constantly changing (although not necessarily quickly or in any particular direction towards 'progress' or 'decadence').

Further, we had always assumed that groups must be clearly bounded in membership, and in a range of characteristics from language to material culture, and so we sought these boundaries. But over many decades anthropologists came to realize it was often very difficult to find the limits of the groups they were studying, and to determine how these were defined, expressed and maintained. It was often unclear who was 'inside' and who 'outside'; limits often proved to be both vague and shifting, while the boundaries of different aspects – such as language or different areas of material culture – did not necessarily coincide with each other. Many facets of material culture might exhibit no boundaries at all, but reveal a continuum of, say, pottery types or language, between peoples who regarded themselves as different from one another. And societies often tended to be internally much more heterogeneous than anticipated. It was all far messier than theory allowed for: gradually it was realized that anthropologists and other scholars had been imposing prior assumptions on the peoples they were studying, by seeking to draw definite edges around named entities and assuming basic homogeneity within those boundaries. American scholars call this the 'cookie-cutter' (in British English, 'pastry-cutter') conception of identities, which obscures the possibility that there may be very vague boundaries, multiple boundaries of different aspects of society, or even no sharp boundaries at all – a continuum. It has become increasingly clear that the 'cookie-cutter' is generally a poor representation of reality.

From the 1960s onwards, the increasingly unsatisfactory existing theoretical framework and methodologies were subject to intense scrutiny, from entirely new perspectives which, as was the case when the older ideas were originally formulated, depended on developments in the wider contemporary cultural and political outlook of Western society. This was itself changing enormously in the aftermath of the Second World War, and particularly with the end of European colonialism. The rise of cultural and national self-consciousness among colonized societies, and the disintegration of the last European overseas empires, discredited long-held imperial ideologies. Exposure of the idea of 'inevitable progress' as an ideological construct, the rejection of assumptions of white racial superiority and of corresponding denigratory beliefs about others, demanded close scrutiny of social theories which hitherto had widely been taken for granted. The arrival of substantial new ethnic groups from the former colonized world in countries such as Britain and France also put the spotlight on relations between different races and cultures.

Meanwhile, in the United States, there was a realization among social scientists that the American 'melting pot' was not functioning as expected. Immigrants were not, as assumed, simply abandoning their own traditions and identities and becoming generic Americans; on the contrary, while adopting much of the framework of American culture, many groups were simultaneously maintaining and even strengthening their sense of separate identity within the United States, manifested in the re-emphasis on 'hyphenated Americans' since the 1960s (Native-American, African-American, and so on). Recognition of this prompted renewed interest in how human identity-groups arise and why they persist.

All these developments led to a profound re-evaluation of existing theories. It was realized that the terminology we use – indeed any terminology – reflects a particular set of values and assumptions about the world, and ideas such as 'cultures', 'nations' or 'races', while related to observable human reality, are nevertheless not natural or inevitable categories, but reflect ideology. This resulted in a new awareness of the inherent Western supremacism of ideas, terms and usages such as 'tribe' and 'primitive', and of notions of progress and timelessness. The idea that other societies around the world could be labelled as 'primitive' and treated as essentially static and 'backward' was attacked as a construct highly convenient to colonial regimes.

It became clear that Western scholarship, from its self-appointed privileged position, had tended to impose its own ideas and judgements on other groups, according to notions derived from colonialist ideologies, and often taking little or no account of the views of the peoples in question. A notorious example of this has been the labelling of all native American peoples as 'Indians', arising from Columbus's prejudices about the conformation of the world and where he had arrived on crossing the Atlantic. Although the peoples concerned had nothing to do with India, and exhibited enormous cultural variation, the imposed blanket name stuck in Western minds.

Recognition of these biases inherent in the ways we have hitherto thought about other societies – in our own world and also in the remote past – has led to attempts to approach the questions in new ways which seek to escape the colonialist past. Of course, *any* alternative formulation will itself be rooted in one or another ideological framework, as there is no 'neutral and objective' approach available to us; we are all embedded in one cultural context or another. However, it is now at least possible to discuss such frameworks more openly, and to assess their implications for our models of human societies. Some current approaches are outlined in the next chapter.

IMPLICATIONS FOR ARCHAEOLOGY, AND FOR THE INSULAR ANCIENT CELTS

Recent revolutions in our understanding of contemporary human societies, in anthropology and other social sciences, have had an equally profound impact on how we envisage peoples in the past. The realization that 'primitive' peoples can and do change internally, and often engage in complex interactions with neighbours, completely discredits the old assumptions that change must mean migration or invasion (or indeed passive acculturation from a 'superior' neighbouring culture such as Greece or Rome). Indeed, a consideration of documentary history shows that general continuity of population does not preclude rapid and profound culture change. Numerically small incursions can have large effects, as the Roman and Norman invasions demonstrate; but equally profound changes can come about with no invasions or migrations at all, as a result of external contacts (e.g. the spread of Christianity) or may be generated locally (the industrial revolution).

In the case of the insular Iron Age, as indigenous development became more thinkable, richer archaeological evidence pointed more and more towards continuity with contact and change as the best conception of the period, and made substantial continental invasions less and less plausible. The most influential attack on the old migrationist model was made by Hodson in the early 1960s. This emphasized instead the basic continuity and distinctiveness of Iron Age British archaeology, although the argument was still framed in terms of archaeological 'cultures' (notably the indigenous 'Little Woodbury culture' and the late, Gallic-inspired 'Aylesford-Swarling culture'). The new pictures of the Iron Age which followed in the 1970s and after were heavily influenced by wider movements in archaeology, which was more consciously drawing on other disciplines and attempting to be more 'scientific': for example, the work of scholars such as Barry Cunliffe applied ideas from geographical theory to archaeological data. It was a major advance in understanding, but still tended to equate archaeological distribution patterns simply with social formations and, in the Late Iron Age, with the named peoples we encounter in classical texts.

However, the discrediting of established ideas about clearly definable and neatly bounded 'cultures' in the present undermines the idea that they existed in the past. In fact, it is now clear that the very methods which archaeologists found so valuable when initially mapping out the shape of the past in time and space – comparing and classifying artefact types and plotting the distributions of these types on maps – made the past *appear* to consist of just such presupposed homogeneous, bounded entities, even where, on examination, the data actually consists of a continuum of finely graded variations in artefacts and of indistinct distributions. Archaeological cultures have traditionally been seen as monolithic, defined on the basis of the presence (or absence) of particular traits, sometimes a very small number indeed (for example, of certain pottery types and a few other artefacts). It now seems that such archaeological 'cultures' have been largely the products of the minds and expectations of archaeologists, rather than unambiguously observable realities: archaeologists have sought and emphasized similarity and uniformity, and have selectively played down variation, drawing boundaries where they did not necessarily exist. It is now quite clear that archaeologists have been applying their own version of the 'cookie-cutter' approach to defining human groups.

In all respects, then, the basic assumptions underpinning the ways in which we think about human identity groups, in the present and in the past, have all been seriously questioned in recent times. What new framework can we put in place of the old?

4 CURRENT IDEAS ON ETHNICITY, AND THE INSULAR ANCIENT CELTS

Currently, the concept of the 'ethnic group' has been adopted as an acceptable alternative to the more loaded terms used to describe human groupings: we have seen that words like 'race' or 'culture' are seriously compromised. The key change is that the definition of such groups now depends not on outsiders such as anthropologists, but on self-definition, by the group in question. It expresses the recognition that other people's own views of their identity and affiliations should be given prominence. On this definition, true ethnic groups must have an 'ethnonym', a *self*-name: names imposed by outsiders do not count, unless they are taken up by those who are labelled. Hence the rejection of imposed labels such as American 'Indian', a classic example already mentioned of the application of quite erroneous assumptions by an alien culture according to its own beliefs (Columbus was not in India, as he thought), and one which groups people together in ways which may have no local meaning at all (the 'Indians' were not a single, self-aware cultural grouping and had no one collective name for themselves). As we have seen, there is no evidence that the peoples who started to see themselves as 'Celtic' after 1700 ever shared such a sense of joint identity, or a single ethnonym, at any earlier date. So, is someone a Celt if they don't know they are a Celt? According to this view, they cannot be so called.

Ethnicity, like all such abstractions, has problems of definition, as we shall see, but it is currently the most useful approach. Notwithstanding the problems of exactly how we define them, how are such identities constituted, and how do they work? There are many competing theories and interpretations of ethnicity. The definition of an ethnic identity used here is that recently proposed by Siân Jones, on whose recent book much of the following discussion of ethnicity is based:

... that aspect of a person's self-conceptualization which results from identification with a broader group in opposition to others, on the basis of *perceived* cultural difference and/or *perceived* common descent.

(Jones 1997, p. xiii. The italics are mine.)

Those group identities which currently we call 'ethnicities' are extraordinarily varied in nature, and often not readily separable from other dimensions of identity such as rank, gender and notably certain religions (e.g. Islam and Judaism). I am using the term 'ethnic group' in the broadest sense to include marginal cases which are certainly group identities, but arguably distinctive enough to count as ethnicities ('Yorkshireman' might be a good case to discuss!). We can certainly say what they are not: as we have seen, we have to abandon the common, simple mental model of sharp-edged, internally homogeneous mosaic tiles which persist essentially unchanged through time. Also controversial is to treat modern national identities under the same general heading: some believe that modern nationalism is not really the same in kind as ethnicity, although of course there are powerful similarities and connections. I do not distinguish sharply between the two here.

ETHNICITIES IN PRACTICE – AND AS PRACTICE

How, then, do ethnic identities such as 'Celticness' develop, and why? The theoretical approach favoured here gets around the problems of defining their nature through drawing up a checklist of characteristics and delineating boundaries round them, by rejecting the notion of such group identities as fixed *things* and instead seeing them as *processes*. Ethnicity is lived out, constantly reaffirmed and, as we shall see, updated. The roots of ethnic identities are not to be found in mystical 'spirit' or unchanging 'essence', belief in which is an aspect, not a source, of identity. Instead of chasing elusive abstractions, this approach seeks the origins and nature of ethnicity in the very nature of our lives, in those patterns of social practices through which society is constituted. It is especially attractive because it makes comprehensible the bewildering complexity of ethnicities, their mutability and their elusiveness.

Human groups work out for themselves practical routines of everyday life, depending on their environment and economy. Division of labour, and the giving or denying to individuals or subgroups of access to resources (e.g. through gender or status divisions), are reflected in the rules and ways of doing things which people work out for themselves. These guide everything from the ways in which people speak to each other and arrange buildings and other social spaces to the artefacts they make, how they use them and what they come to symbolize, their cosmo-logical beliefs and rites of passage (such as burial rites). This culture which they create and *live out* (rather than *possess*) is generally taken for granted: it is 'what the world is like', and for the most part below the hori-zon of conscious thought. Under these circumstances, people living in such groups have no active sense of special identity in the world at all; it may be said that the question of ethnicity simply does not arise. The African people known to others as LoWiili have no sense of corporate identity, and no name for themselves. Ethnic awareness does not develop unless there are reasons for it to do so; and those reasons, it seems, invari-ably centre on contacts with others who are perceived to be different.

Interesting things happen when societies suddenly find themselves in contact with strangers who do things differently. This is at least startling, and may be shocking, even where the groups are in peaceful contact. Both groups will focus on those traits in the other which are different, and apparently bizarre, in terms of their own ways. These may be glaringly obvious ('They' may speak an unintelligible language, or dress 'strangely', or behave in an incomprehensible fashion), or the cause of incredulity and discussion may apparently be features which to third parties seem quite mundane or trivial. A particular focus is often dietary habits: what do 'They' eat, and how? A classic example of this is to be seen in the tell-tale nicknames which the English and French gave each other in the eighteenth century – 'frog-eaters' and '*rosbifs*', from mutual stereotypes about dining habits considered as both characteristic and odd (eating of the unpalatable versus crude gluttony).

Such encounters and reactions have two effects: encountering a differ-ent 'Them' makes a group suddenly conscious of 'Us', which raises the question of who 'We' are, and what defines and differentiates 'Us' from 'Them'. This throws the spotlight on those aspects of 'Our' culture from which 'They' differ. Whatever the foci of perceived difference, they are thrown into conscious discussion and 'Our' ways of doing these things may then be deliberately elaborated into symbols of difference which demarcate who is 'Us' and who belongs to 'Them'. The particular range of symbols chosen can include anything from a language to features of dress or certain patterns of religious or other behaviour. The range of symbols is as varied as human societies are complex, because they depend on the particular features of the societies in contact at that time, the nature and circumstances of contact, and the ways the groups involved respond to one another, all of which are impossible to predict. Ethnicity, then, is historically contingent to a massive degree. The identities which may arise in such contexts, each of which is unique, manifest themselves in amazingly varied ways, which then continue to shift according to developing circumstances.

A group will define itself by choosing a self-name, or ethnonym. An existing word meaning something like 'the people' or 'the community' may come to have a specific group-identifying meaning (e.g. *Cymry*, *Deutsch*). Ethnicity can become intensely important, where groups are in direct competition and conflict, or where there is only a *perception* of threat (whether of military aggression, or of cultural or political domination) from the Other.

People may possess more than one ethnic identity. For example, I feel myself to have a number of quasi-ethnic identities (regional to ethnic, national and trans-national), which seem to me to be neatly 'nested' like Russian dolls (figs 10–11). Other cases may be more complex. It is

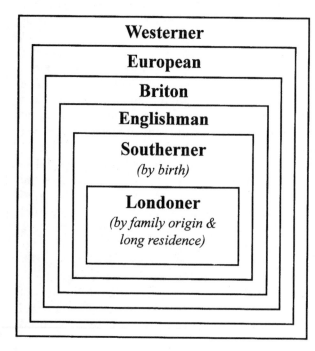

Westerner

European

Briton

Englishman

Southerner
(by birth)

Londoner
(by family origin & long residence)

10. *My own group identities, which I perceive as neatly nested. 'Londoner' and 'Southerner' are arguably not ethnic identities, although they occasionally feel very much like them when one is an 'expatriate' living in the North-East of England! People's various identities do not always so neatly resemble 'Russian dolls'.*

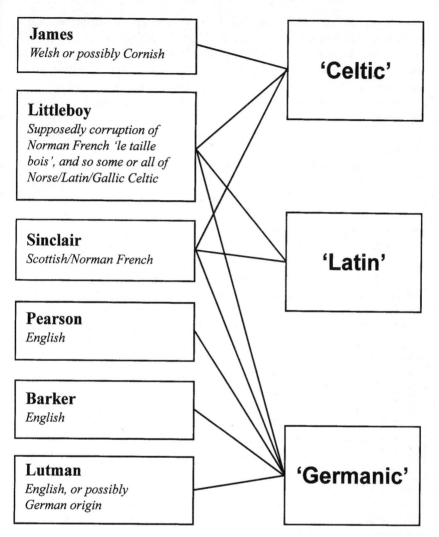

James
Welsh or possibly Cornish

Littleboy
Supposedly corruption of Norman French 'le taille bois', and so some or all of Norse/Latin/Gallic Celtic

Sinclair
Scottish/Norman French

Pearson
English

Barker
English

Lutman
English, or possibly German origin

'Celtic'

'Latin'

'Germanic'

11. *My 'ethnic ancestry' according to the family names of my recent forebears, as it would be expressed in simplistic genealogical terms. I know almost nothing of my origins beyond the last four generations or so, apart from some limited family traditions and inference from traditional 'ethnic' or national affiliations of these attested family names. These would seem to suggest a mixed 'Celtic', 'Germanic' and perhaps 'Latin' background.*

le to hold parallel identities – as in modern dual-nationality ₁gements – or even patterns of apparently contradictory identities. ₁ul, for example, a Greek-speaking Jew from the city-state of Tarsus in wₙₐt is now Turkey, was also a Roman citizen; here is a person with no less than three cross-cutting ethnic identities (in at least a loose sense).

Ethnic identities, born of social practices, are largely expressed through them. Of course symbols are often very important to group identity, especially where it is too large be directly experienced as a whole and becomes an 'imagined community'. They become more important as a means of recognizing 'Us' (an obvious example is the flag of the United States, which is the subject of national reverence as a symbol of 'American-ness' to a degree which puzzles many Europeans). However, it is in *action* that ethnic or national identity is actually lived, including saluting the flag, but in a host of less formal circumstances too.

Typically, we do not spend much of our time thinking about our identities; they are something which is brought to the fore only when needed. Ethnic identities are only expressed in contexts and at times when contact with others is an issue, from dealings in the marketplace to travelling among 'foreign' communities or fighting wars. One can argue that most of the time the average ethnic group has no actual existence; it only 'appears' when individuals and groups need to be conscious of their ethnicity and to manifest it in action. In my own case, each of my multiple identities is important to me, but most of the time they are not 'active'. I only think about, and actively 'live' one or another in particular contexts: for example, living in Durham, I am sometimes acutely aware of being a Southerner; visiting Scotland, of my Englishness; when in America, I can become *awfully* British, and may also be very conscious that, culturally, I have more in common with fellow Europeans in Paris or Naples than with fellow Anglophones in New York, Madison or Fresno (this last is an illustration that language similarities and differences are no simple determinant of one's sense of identity).

Because, if it appears at all, ethnic identity is constantly generated and regenerated at the points of contact between more than one society, and because the societies involved, and the patterns of their interaction, are constantly changing through time, then the manifestations of ethnicity are constantly shifting too. And, although ethnicities are widely perceived as being 'in the blood' – identities with which people are ingrained from birth – there is often a considerable gap between the ways such identities portray themselves in terms of boundaries and membership, and the actual experiences of people involved. In practice it is to varying degrees possible to change one's group affiliations, by adding, dropping or exchanging them. Individuals or groups can cross at least some ethnic boundaries. It becomes possible to appreciate why defining such identities is so difficult.

Although, by definition, ethnic groups feel themselves to be internally 'the same', in fact they may be quite heterogeneous. For example, the Pathans of Afghanistan and Pakistan constitute a self-aware ethnic group, but exhibit considerable internal differences between constituent elements: their sense of shared identity is based on common organization in certain areas of social relations which are considered to be of fundamental importance, notably rules of hospitality, the conduct of public affairs and the seclusion of domestic life. Commonality in these marks Pathans out from others, and their differences in other aspects of life are not important to their sense of shared identity.

Conversely, while apparently disparate groups of people may regard one another as part of the same group, peoples who appear to outsiders to be closely similar may regard themselves as very different. A stark example is provided by several of the peoples of former Yugoslavia – the Croats, Serbs and Bosnian Muslims – who speak the same language and share many historical roots, but ferociously contest the primarily religion-based ethnic boundaries between them.

Yugoslavia makes the case that ethnic groups are often not sharply bounded in all aspects of culture: many traits may be common both sides of an ethnic divide. The various dimensions of identity – e.g. language and material culture – may each have different boundaries, and these particular boundaries may themselves be vague. For example, the archaeologist Ian Hodder investigated the material expression of identity among the modern people of the Baringo district of Kenya, looking at dress and other artefacts used, language, etc. He showed that there *were* clear material cultural distinctions between groups, maintained in a variety of artefact types, but not all; other categories were used both sides of group boundaries, exhibiting a continuum. Future archaeologists will find it hard to judge which distributions of artefacts correspond with social group boundaries, and which do not.

Ethnic groups commonly seek legitimacy by claiming deep historical roots, which to a greater or lesser degree are invented. Take, for example, the case of the Romans and their origin myths. In a 'prequel' to the foundation of the city itself by Romulus and Remus, the Romans claimed that their line went back further, as Latium had been settled by the Trojan prince Aeneas and his followers, who had escaped the sack of Troy. Set down by Virgil in his *Aeneid*, Rome's national epic, the story gave the upstart Romans an ancestral link to peoples and figures in the 'bible' of the culturally dominant Greek world, Homer's *Iliad*. (Julius Caesar claimed direct descent from Aeneas, who was son of the goddess Venus, and ancestral pedigrees do not come better than that!) Such a pedigree was felt to be vital if Rome was to be truly included in the circle of Mediterranean civilization. The Roman example was later copied in England, in the tradition regarding the origins of Britain which preceded ideas about Celts. This sought to derive the name of Britain from another Trojan, called Brutus, descendant of Prince Aeneas, who was alleged to have settled in the island. Just as in the case of the *Aeneid*, this would of course provide Britain with the prestige of a good classical pedigree in a Renaissance world which venerated Graeco-Roman culture.

Many, sometimes the majority, may feel weakly attached to a nominal identity. Ethnicity may be regarded as less important than the other major dimensions of identity within their social world (e.g. gender, religion or rank). It may be that a strong sense of group identity is confined to certain parts of society which consider it important (e.g. politically active urban groups, while rural populations may regard such questions as of little relevance or interest to their daily concerns). For example, Irish identity is today much more of an immediate, daily, conscious, passionate concern to nationalists in Northern Ireland (who are in direct confrontation with equally passionate Protestant loyalists) than it is to many people in Dublin.

Once an ethnic identity appears, it seems that it will only continue to exist so long as the group perceives a need for it and makes an effort to maintain it. Major changes in a group's internal circumstances may lead to dissipation, fission or fusion with neighbours, as the appearance of new, more alien 'Others' prompts them to find common cause expressed in a new sense of inclusive identity. If a group is no longer in contact, and especially in contest, with Others, the importance of its sense of ethnic difference and solidarity may decline as other, internal issues take centre stage again. This seems pretty clearly the case with 'Britishness' in the late twentieth century. Even where the dominant axis of cultural self-definition remains apparently the same over time (as for centuries the English were preoccupied with the French and the Scots), the patterns of contact, and the internal nature of the Other, all continually change, demanding modifications in the definition and expression of ethnic difference.

These cases illustrate that ethnic identity is not static, because over time it is lived out by different generations of people, in different historical circumstances; and because the ways it is expressed respond to shifts in relations with outside groups against which it is defined. Since ethnicity is a set of beliefs and practices which must be learned, expressed and reproduced by social action, so – with the passing of the generations, with local, internal social changes within the group, economic or technological developments or religious realignment – as the actors themselves are replaced, so inevitably will the ethnicity they act out undergo change. Ethnic and national identities *feel* 'natural', and all but eternal and unchanging; they are seen in terms of the 'spirit' of the people, their connectedness within the community and not least with the past. Yet identities actually exhibit a mix of continuity and innovation. Even where specific, named ethnic groups can be shown to persist for centuries, the changes they undergo due to continual redefinition of themselves from generation to generation mean that remote ancestors and distant descendants who share the same group name, if they could meet, might not recognize each other as the same.

The symbolic meanings attached to aspects of culture which make them expressive of ethnic identity – such as language or particular categories of artefact – are not fixed, then, but open to redefinition. Such symbols may last, and become elaborated into icons, but they can also be abandoned: many Scots now feel that the 'biscuit-tin-Highlander', for example, created in the nineteenth century, is no longer a favoured symbol of contemporary Scottishness. Even the most revered symbols do not stay exactly unchanging: historical places, shrines and sacred texts may seem constant, but the values and interpretations ascribed to them change as the interpreters change generation by generation.

Similarly, while many long-standing aspects of Irish culture such as indigenous language, literature and musical traditions retain great importance, much of what characterizes Irishness today is very different from the Irishness of fifty years ago. Notably, the Catholic Church dominated mid-century Irish life, culture and politics, but has lost much of its importance now; many Irish people today see their society as a sophisticated, secular, industrial democracy. Catholicism had long been closely linked with Irish identity, not least as an important expression of difference from the Protestant- and English-dominated colonial power,

Britain. A major part of the reason for the eclipse of the Church following Irish independence is the removal of the outside cultural pressure which gave it such particular symbolic value under colonial rule. Under these very different circumstances a couple of generations after throwing off British control, in the context of a federalizing Europe in which Ireland can be an equal partner and not a colony, Irishness has developed a new, more relaxed self-confidence (except in the North, where identity in the island has still been contested to the death in recent decades), and is abandoning some cultural symbols, modifying others, and adding new ones.

Finally, in the case of some identities it is not clear whether they are/were ethnic, national, religious, or primarily about status within a wider population; often they partake of two or more of these dimensions. For example, the Spartiates of ancient Sparta were both a ruling élite and, in origin, an identity group, dominating the ethnically separate Helots.

To summarize these complex features:

- *Ethnicity is a cultural construct*, and may have little to do with the 'real' historical background(s) of the individuals and sub-groups concerned. Seen from the inside, ethnicity is about what people *believe* their identity is, and where it came from.
- *Ethnic identities are not static things which people possess.* Ethnicity is not a *thing*, which can be pinned down, defined and described; it is a complex *social process*. Ethnicity is not something you *possess*, it is something that you *live out*, affirming and recreating it through time. This very different conceptualization of ethnic identities allows us to make sense of the often bewildering complexity and intangibility encountered when studying such groups today.
- *People may not have an ethnic identity at all.*
- *Ethnic identities are more about perceived difference from others, than about similarities.* They are largely about awareness of *difference* from other groups with which they are in contact; their genesis, their nature, and their continued maintenance are therefore closely related to specific historical circumstances.
- *Ethnic identities may be multiple.* People always have multiple identities (gender, social rank, religion, etc.), often including more than one ethnic identity in the broader sense.
- *An ethnic identity may be more important to some than to others.* Adherence to a named identity may be highly variable within a

society, for example according to social position, or how far one encounters outsiders.

- *Ethnic identities are rarely homogeneous.* They may exhibit considerable internal complexity.
- *Conversely, apparent cultural similarity is no sure indicator of shared ethnicity.*
- *Ethnic identities are rarely sharply bounded.*
- *Ethnic identities are fluid and situational: they are not expressed all the time.*
- *Ethnic identities are constantly changing,* in greater or lesser ways. As these change, so does the nature of the ethnic identity. It may be destroyed, deliberately by human action (genocide) or inadvertently, by disease (the fate of many Native American peoples after contact with Europeans) or natural catastrophes such as climate change; it may fade out because it is no longer needed in current circumstances; or it may be continued.
- *The symbols of ethnicity are not fixed,* in nature or value.
- *Ethnic groups commonly seek legitimacy through claiming deep historical roots,* which may be fictionalized, or at least highly partisan, representations of the past.
- *Development of each ethnicity depends on specific historical circumstances.* Ethnicity is historically contingent to a massive degree.

IDENTIFYING ETHNIC GROUPS IN THE PAST: THE INSULAR IRON AGE

As we have seen, ethnicity is a subject fraught with difficulty even in the present, where we can speak to people about their personal conception of their own identities and observe how they actually express them. For the remote past, before we have documentary sources, the fluid and situational nature of ethnic identity makes it very difficult for archaeology to identify *specific* ethnicities directly: since they are largely exhibited only at certain times, as transient acts and practices, most manifestations of ethnicity (e.g. language) leave no archaeological trace. Even where there are rich remains of artefacts and specific patterns of domestic or ritual behaviour on settlements and in cemeteries, while we can be sure notions of identity have had impact on the record, which identities are represented? Gender, age, status, religion and other dimensions are all likely to have played a part, making it hard to distinguish specifically ethnic referents. Even if ethnicity was expressed materially, quite mundane items may have been invested with deep symbolic value, in ways which are hard for archaeologists to spot. For instance, one of the distinguishing marks of the identity of Roman soldiers during the third century AD (an identity, incidentally, which had both ethnic and status aspects) seems to have been the 'no-nonsense' plainness of their garments compared with those of other privileged Roman males, women and foreigners. Even if clear material distinctions once existed (and as we have seen, clear, sharp boundaries are often absent), the traces of these complex patterns which get buried for archaeologists to find are both incomplete and blurred by the vagaries of processes of deposition and preservation. All this makes defining 'peoples' and ascribing ethnic names dangerous, if not foolhardy.

However, although it is proving more difficult to identify *specific* ethnicities in the past than we have liked to think (under the old, simplistic 'cookie-cutter' approach), it is possible to apply our general understanding of human behaviour and cultural formations to the patterns observed in archaeological contexts such as the insular Iron Age, and so to draw conclusions about plausible presence and *scales* of ethnic identity.

In Britain and Ireland, the general patterns which archaeology is revealing, overwhelmingly of small-scale, short-range social life, and of great regional diversity, are irreconcilable with the idea of one unified ethnic identity we can call 'Celtic'. Our much-improved understanding of small-scale human societies in general, and of the fine detail of the remains left by insular peoples in particular, makes it unlikely that there were any very large-scale, self-conscious ethnic communities *at all* until some county-sized, fairly unstable entities appeared in the south and east of Britain in the Late Iron Age. There was no island-wide notion of ethnic 'Britishness' or 'Irishness' either, let alone awareness of overarching 'Celticness'. Very large-scale identities such as the recent national ones of Ireland and Britain probably could not have existed until at least the Roman period, because such large-scale identities depend on two things: an equivalent large scale of social interaction, and the presence of other, major, clearly different groupings against which major population groups felt the collective need to differentiate themselves. The move towards larger-scale societies in Gaul in the later Iron Age may have helped generate a nascent sense of shared British identity among those southern groups in contact with Gaul; and the sudden appearance of a huge alien power on the scene – the Roman empire – certainly seems to have encouraged development of at least regional identities within the isles. But I shall argue that even at the end of the Roman period, the group identities we encounter are at most regional; the notions of common 'Britishness' in Britain, and common 'Irishness' in Ireland, were weakly developed, or really still things of the future.

Even in those areas where self-aware, named entities were appearing in the British Isles before the Late Iron Age (and there were probably populations with no collective identity describable as an ethnicity), these were very different from modern mass national identities: they were most likely ill defined, both geographically and in terms of adherence of the wider population to them. It looks as though the named entities were largely – perhaps entirely – the creations of individuals or dynasties, who, by military or political means, established power over, and named, 'peoples'; that peoples did not create kings, but kings created 'peoples', who may or may not have accepted and made a commitment to an identity imposed from above, which then became an ethnicity.

Current interpretations also suggest that the Iron Age populations of the isles had not recently radiated from one, quite small and homogeneous source (in which case they might be expected to be, and to remain, culturally close, and perhaps to retain an original sense of ethnic unity); rather, they descended in parallel from a spectrum of earlier insular populations (although with many meetings, mergings, crossovers and divisions).

Under such circumstances, 'Celtic', or indeed even 'British' or 'Irish' are not especially useful even as loose cultural terms, because these abstractions mask the apparently real situation of many autonomous local or regional communities, or in some areas and periods even a continuum of farming families with little overall group structure beyond short-range kinship links, and few signs of any sense of particular unitary identity. More fundamentally, the differences within each island are, arguably, greater than the similarities across them.

The traditional emphasis on the presumed essential cultural similarity between the insular Iron Age peoples, then, may well be highly misleading; it is largely an *expectation* derived from general patterns of thinking and specific notions about Celts, explored above, which led earlier generations of archaeologists to look for it in ways which produced the right kinds of results. But once this implicit expectation is highlighted, it becomes apparent that the evidence can be understood in quite different terms: of essential *difference*, of multiple, autonomous traditions, whose similarities, undoubted but not universal, arose from mutual contact and *convergence*, not from inherited commonalities of shared roots. The archaeological evidence strongly suggests that a 'multiple traditions' perspective is viable, and may prove a more useful description than the traditional 'normative' one. At the very least, it provides us with an alternative, so that we now have a pair of competing models to test against the evidence. The usefulness and validity of the normative 'variations on a Celtic theme' model for the Iron Age must be demonstrated and not (as hitherto has commonly been the case) assumed at the outset.

To understand the insular Iron Age better, we must recognize and explore the complexity in the data and painstakingly look at the patterns of variation, area by area, trying to tease out such characteristics, differences and boundaries as there may have been. We must offer prehistory the same courtesy that we offer later periods of insular history. To understand the islands in, say, the sixteenth century, we know that we must consider the various nations (and indeed their regions) separately, if we are to understand them jointly. In the context of the Iron Age, then, terms like 'Irish' and 'British' are little more than geographical locators, not necessarily any more indicative of a specific culture or identity than the term 'European' today, i.e., not an ethnonym – at least, not yet. If 'Celtic' has any utility at all for the Iron Age, then it is analogous to a term like 'Western Christendom' for Europe five centuries ago – a label for a geographical cluster of highly varied cultures with some important shared characteristics and values, largely acquired through mutual contacts, but with no sense of overall, shared, ethnic or national identity. The implications of these views for the histories of the isles are discussed in more detail in the next chapter.

The foregoing has outlined an approach to the question of group identity in the past from anthropology and sociology and from developments in archaeology. It has not made significant mention of linguistics, with which the story of the insular Celts began, nor of biology, with which Celtic discourse was closely entwined in the nineteenth century. The reason for this is that archaeology (especially prehistory) and the fields of philology and linguistics have diverged greatly in their philosophy, and have very little contact; the scholarly communities rarely speak to each other. Archaeologists are also very wary of biological approaches to earlier populations and groupings, both given the history of racist manipulation of such data and because the gulf of understanding between the two disciplines is even wider than that between archaeologists and language specialists. Clearly, neither field can be left out of any comprehensive attempt to investigate the subject in hand. What to do?

LANGUAGE

Research on ethnicity in general, and on the archaeology of the insular Iron Age in particular, raises important questions about the role of philology in these discussions. Of course, this is a highly developed discipline very different from my own, but what it says concerns me in both senses of the word, especially the way linguists use the term 'Celt'. Colin Renfrew quotes the philologist Myles Dillon as saying in 1977:

By Celts I mean people who spoke a Celtic dialect, not people who buried their dead in urn-fields or had leaf-shaped swords or any particular kind of pottery. Language is the test. This is not an infallible statement of known truth; it is merely an agreed use of the term upon which linguists insist.

(Renfrew 1987, p. 225)

From my own recent contact with Celtic linguists, such usage is still current. To me, this 'insistence' is simply unacceptable. 'Celt' was originally a group name applied to one or more peoples, *not* a linguistic description, and it is still understood as an ethnonym by most people today. Such a usage by philologists either claims that language is the determinant of identity – which is plainly wrong (English speech, labelled 'Germanic' by linguists, does not mean that Americans are Germans) – or that ethnic names can be appropriated for strictly linguistic usage, which breeds exactly the kind of ambiguity, misunderstanding and confusion that bedevils the whole Celtic issue. It is manifestly obvious, for example, that Celtic identity is not dependent on speaking a Celtic language, otherwise millions of people today who regard themselves as culturally or ethnically Celtic are disqualified (as has been argued elsewhere, language is a common, but not an inevitably determining, component of a particular sense of identity). Of course philologists and linguists need a label for 'speakers of languages we choose to call Celtic', but surely 'Celtic speakers' is unambiguous enough.

Archaeologists have particular grounds for concern over philologists' conclusions about peoples, cultures and historical processes in the context of the Iron Age, because they in part continue to rely on now discredited invasionist ideas and chronologies drawn from archaeology. (As we have seen, these were themselves in part originally constructed on assumptions drawn from early philological work: the danger of circular argument is manifest.) The philologists who first identified the kinship of those languages they called Celtic assumed that they must have spread to the isles through migrations of continental Celts, because they believed languages and named peoples could be simply and unambiguously equated, and because they knew no other mechanisms for this to happen. The dates for these migrations were unclear, but classical writers placed the earliest known Celts in Central Europe around 500 BC and mentioned southward migrations a century later. Early archaeologists believed that they were finding evidence for matching Iron Age migrations into Britain and Ireland, because they, too, knew no other mechanism to explain the similarities they found. Much subsequent philological literature has used archaeological interpretations as a chronological peg on which to hang the hypothetical history of Celtic language development. But there is no solid reason at all to link the appearance of languages now called Celtic with the spread of any particular archaeological 'culture', whether La Tène or any other. In any case, as we have seen, the archaeological basis for this reconstruction based on supposed folk-movements is now discredited. We seem to have a direct conflict between what archaeologists claim the direct physical traces of the period tell us about the insular Iron Age, and what philologists assert the (generally later) linguistic evidence must imply.

Within current understandings of how languages develop, can we not reconcile the archaeological picture, of essential continuity of populations from the Bronze Age rather than mass migrations, with the historically recorded linguistic patterns? Can the demonstrable similarities in the insular Celtic languages be explained *only* by radiation from a common ancestral language, at an earlier time, in a more limited area, as many philologists seem still to argue? This seems to treat languages as though they were Darwinian biological species, which of course they are not. They are not generally as sharply defined as modern 'national' languages seek to be, and can powerfully influence each other directly (a simple illustration of which is that about a fifth of English vocabulary is taken from French/Latin). Such imagery makes me wonder whether much of linguistics – like much of archaeology – still clings to established ideas which are not the only possible truth, and which are actually based on earlier cultural assumptions embedded in scholarship – assumptions deriving from sources such as Pezron's biblical imagery and Victorian ideas on descent and evolution. No doubt, language specialists will have much of interest to say on this issue!

Some have already attempted to reconcile philology and archaeology. Colin Renfrew, drawing on various trends in language studies as well as developments in archaeology, has proposed a very different model, in which the origins of the Celtic tongues of the islands are not to be found in the Iron Age, but much earlier, in the spread of the first farming populations into the islands, around 6,000 years ago (Renfrew 1987, especially chapter 9). The suggestion is that the various Celtic languages of Europe arose and developed in parallel, and in intimate mutual contact, from an early date, and did not arrive from anywhere else at all. The various characteristics of, and differences between, the Celtic tongues and vocabularies are envisaged as arising *in situ* in continental Europe and the isles, not radiating from any central 'homeland'. Could some such model not form the basis for comprehensive explanations encompassing both archaeological and philological evidence?

BIOLOGY AND GENETICS

Hitherto, the discussion has made little reference to biology. As we have seen, especially in the nineteenth century biological data and interpretations were very important in the debate about the Celts, but this approach was compromised and discredited by the long, dark history of racism and eugenics which reached its nadir in Nazi Germany. The realization that identities are not closely tied to biology has also meant that modern genetics has not featured much in modern discussions of the Celts. One's genetic make-up depends unequivocally on one's physical forebears, but cultural affiliation does not. Of course, there is a tendency, often a strong one, for people to chooses their mates from within their own community, but this is very far from being universal now, and there is good reason to think this has always been so. While *notional* biological or 'blood' descent is important to many cultures, it is equally clear that this is often achieved through fictionalization of common ancestry. The relationship between biology and culture is constantly blurred by the mutability of identity and the possibility of adopting new identities – moving to other communities, learning new languages, living in new ways. Thus there is a relationship between genetics and human identity, but a complex one, its nature

with difficulties of theory and method. The scope for misunder-
g, or misrepresentation, remains great.

re specific problem, in the case of the historical origins and development of the insular peoples, is the chronic lack of direct genetic data.
Ideally, to trace the genetic development of, and possible movements
among, the populations of the isles, we would need large samples of good-
quality genetic material taken from human remains recovered from all
areas and across continental Europe at various historical horizons over
the last 3,000 years or more. This would allow good statistical treatment
of patterns of variation and changes in them, which might then be compared with other data to see if they support or contradict ideas about
migration or continuity. In the sixth century BC were there genetic characteristics in Central Europe which were unknown in the islands? Were
such traits widely found in Britain and Ireland by the third century BC? If
so, this would seem to be powerful evidence for movement of people into
the isles, consistent with the 'Celtic migrations' of historical interpretation. If the traits do not appear in Britain, this may provide equally strong
evidence against major migrations. But we do not have such comprehensive data-sets, and are unlikely ever to have them: there remains little
human bone or other tissue from most areas and periods. Unfortunately,
for much of prehistory, the dead were disposed of in ways which leave no
archaeological trace at all. Even where burial did take place, remains were
often cremated, destroying DNA data; where bodies were buried intact,
the DNA is often too decayed to analyse.

In short, for the foreseeable future we are reliant on extrapolation
backwards from present genetic patterns, which brings its own difficulties. For example, as I understand it, it may be possible to establish the
existence of regional genetic patterns in the present population, but it is
not clear that it can be demonstrated with certainty when these came
into being – in AD 1700, AD 400, the pre-Roman Iron Age or the
Neolithic. Some genetic changes are believed to occur at fairly constant
rates, so – assuming the estimates are correct – it may be possible to link
changes to particular historical eras; however, since they are based on
contemporary data, they cannot directly tell us *where* the ancestral
population was at the time of the change.

A final problem which gives geneticists and archaeologists alike pause
for thought when using each other's data is the danger of circularity of
argument, due to mutual incomprehension. For example, biologists, quite
reasonably unfamiliar with the methodological limitations of historical,

linguistic and archaeological evidence (which are themselves hotly disputed), may uncritically take ideas such as Iron Age Celtic migrations as established fact, not appreciating that they may simply be modern theoretical constructs. They may then use such 'facts' to explain features of their genetic data. Archaeologists, historians or linguists, equally unfamiliar with the scientific methodology, may then use this interpretation as evidence to support their own presuppositions.

If the methodological difficulties can be tackled, genetic data may, in the future, prove invaluable in helping us understand the kinds of questions we are dealing with here. However, there is already reason to conclude that the Iron Age peoples of the islands were genetically quite mixed: at least, 2,000 years ago they already included a wide range of Caucasian types. The established 'racial stereotypes' of Britain include the small, dark-haired Welsh, the tall, red-headed Scots, and the lanky, fair-haired English (to which I correspond myself). The latter is often assumed to be the result of Anglo-Saxon and Viking settlement, the others being 'Celtic racial types'. But these stereotypes – including lanky blond Southerners – are already to be found in Roman writers before the 'Germanic invasions', when everyone is supposed to have been Celtic.

5 TOWARDS A NEW ETHNIC HISTORY OF THE ISLES

I t is not enough, as some contemporary archaeological writing does, simply to subject the status quo to critique and then walk away, having revealed (to one's own satisfaction, at least) the inherent contradictions and bankruptcy of established thinking. We have to offer alternative views of how the Celts fit into the wider ethnic and national history of the archipelago. The sketch which follows is provisional, often conjectural, and (like established views) inevitably an oversimplification. However, it aims to produce a plausible reconstruction of how people living in Ireland and Britain have seen their own identities through time, from the Iron Age to the present. It draws on intensive modern research into an ever-expanding body of evidence from the islands themselves, and also into how human societies actually work, rather than on archaic or untested popular assumptions about how they 'should' work.

This alternative account concentrates on the early phases of the story, which are not only less well known than the history of the last few centuries, but also crucial to the central theme of the origins and development of identities in the islands. In particular, they constitute the critical period when general Celticness in the isles was supposedly established. The contrast of the reconstruction offered here with the traditional 'history of the Celtic world' will rapidly become apparent. The latter is a story of fragmentation and reduction, from peripheral membership of the Europe-wide, Iron Age 'Celtic commonwealth' to the survival in the islands of the culture that was obliterated in most of Europe at the hands of the Romans. The subsequent further depredations of Germanic Anglo-Saxons and Vikings are seen as leaving the surviving Celtic peoples as embattled remnants in distant islands and mountain fastnesses. The new model suggested here turns this image almost on its head. It traces the *general* (and multiple) roots of insular cultures back at least into the later Bronze Age, while at the same time arguing that the coming together of the *specific* self-aware groupings which are familiar to us – such as the 'Irish', 'British' and 'Celts' – was later, sometimes very much later, than is usually assumed.

The model envisages the Iron Age isles not as a peripheral backwater of continental Celticity but as areas with their own manifold regional traditions, which, to varying degrees at different times, looked across the waters of the Irish Sea, the Channel and the North Sea to neighbouring lands, engaging in two-way traffic in ideas, goods and *some* people who, intermittently and in an *ad hoc* manner, were added to the map of the isles (see fig. 2 on pp. 14–15). Distant contacts across the water were often easier to maintain than closer ones across the land, owing to the difficulties of the terrain. These external contacts were sometimes so intense and intimate that some insular regions, such as south-east Britain in the first century BC, Argyll in the sixth century AD or Dublin in the eleventh, had more in common with their maritime neighbours than with other communities on the same island. And these are patterns which, arguably, have repeated or persisted throughout history down to the present day. Neither of the two major islands, then, was a distinctive monolithic cultural, political or ethnic entity at any time in the past, as they still are not today. There never was a pristine cultural or ethnic uniformity ('Celtic' or anything else) across the archipelago, but always multiple traditions, undergoing contest and change.

THE LATE BRONZE AGE TO THE END OF THE MIDDLE IRON AGE (c. 1000–150 BC)

During later prehistory, how did people in the archipelago think of themselves? What kinds of identities did they possess? Since they were preliterate, so that no accounts of them exist before the definite (if rather suspect) literary evidence begins to arrive from the Graeco-Roman world, when Britain at least was already in contact with the Roman empire, we are forced to rely on clues from archaeology.

Inferring from the patterns of archaeological evidence deposited during the last millennium BC, we can say that people of the Late Bronze Age and earlier Iron Age societies in the British Isles typically lived by planting crops, tending herds and managing woodlands. The great ceremonial monuments of the Neolithic period and Early and Middle Bronze Ages (from around 4000 BC to around 1500 BC) had been generally abandoned, for reasons unknown. Landscapes of the last millennium BC bear traces of a growing sedentary population. We have no direct data, but there is no reason to doubt that most, perhaps all, of the populations of the isles were already speaking dialects (probably not all mutually comprehensible) that we now classify as members of the Celtic family.

The Late Bronze Age and earlier Iron Age are considered together because the boundary between them is largely a convenient artificial distinction made by archaeologists: the introduction of iron technology, over a few generations around 800 BC, did not mark a sudden revolution in the routines of life in the countryside. The common Iron Age patterns of round or ovoid buildings, pits and earthworks grow directly out of the Late Bronze Age, and much of the mat-erial culture, from farming regimes to regional pottery traditions, also reflects such continuity. Hillforts, too, were often first built before the coming of iron.

People are mostly attested by expanding systems of land boundaries and growing numbers of farming settlements. Where settlement patterns are detectable (and in many regions, notably in Ireland, they are hard to find), they consist of dispersed farmsteads, hamlets or villages, and in some areas hillforts of various sizes. However, there is very little sign of 'infrastructure' denoting large-scale social organization, or of major sites serving the joint religious, political or economic needs of regional communities. The rash of hillfort-building seen in some regions may well have been occasioned by the appearance of small-scale self-aware units in competition with one another, which might qualify as 'ethnic groups'. For example, the famous hillfort of Maiden Castle in Dorset grew and was enormously elaborated during the Early and Middle Iron Age, at the expense of its neighbours. But the erratic history of most hillforts probably reflects the transience and instability of these groupings which, we may suppose, typically appeared, merged and vanished within a few generations. Even the big Wessex forts do not appear to bespeak political units more than a few tens of miles on a side, with populations up to a few thousand. Other areas show no such 'centralizing' trends even on this modest scale. Kin groups or clans were probably the largest social formations.

One of the striking features of settlement patterns is their great diversity from region to region, while other aspects of material culture also betray as much variation as similarity across the island – e.g. between pottery-using and non-pottery-using regions. The map of cultural remains often appears as a highly varied continuum, with an almost fractal-like quality of local variation in terms of what people made and used, and how they used it. All this seems to suggest that human life and sense of identity were overwhelmingly small-scale, local and 'short-range', the farmers largely self-sufficient and in our terms materially impoverished (although this does not preclude society from having been culturally rich and complex). In some areas there are not even trackways between farms and through field-systems, suggesting that large-scale exchange between groups (e.g. driving flocks to central markets) was not yet important. However, there was always a need for *some* outside exchange, sometimes very long-distance, to acquire vital materials not available in many areas, from salt to metals. The peoples of the archipelago were by no means completely isolated from one another.

These relatively tenuous contact networks nevertheless reached across the seas as much as across the islands, to embrace the peoples of the nearer continent. They will have involved small-scale movements of people, involved in diplomatic, religious, military and economic transactions, engaging in competition and conflict, establishing personal links or maintaining long-standing kinship connections. People surely transferred across the waters in all directions, temporarily or permanently, leavening and modifying social patterns but not revolutionizing them through mass migration, expulsion or slaughter and replacement. It was through such contacts that new ways and ideas, from iron technology to – almost half-way through the pre-Roman Iron Age – La Tène-style metalwork, were adopted in some areas, the significance of which is discussed below.

But how did people come together and organize themselves? As we have seen, in most areas the settlement record shows little indication of large-scale groupings; nor is there much, if any, evidence for elaborate social hierarchy or specialized classes before the Middle Iron Age, and much later in many regions. There are no special graves, and few signs of the kinds of splendid personal equipment which we associate with 'warrior aristocracies' or priesthoods. For most of the Iron Age, households were the main units of life and production, with little evidence of social stratification between them. Activities such as warfare and religious rites were engaged in by people at every settlement, and were not concentrated in the hands of select classes. If by no means pacific, societies were apparently relatively egalitarian. It seems, then, that the archetype of 'Celtic' social structure as often conceived does not fit the archaeology of Britain or Ireland for most of the Iron Age. As we shall see, in *some* areas individuals began to mark themselves out through personal finery from the Middle Iron Age onwards, but it is only in south-eastern England at the end of the pre-Roman Iron Age that we see highly visible differences in wealth and power, reflecting sharply divided social classes.

The evidence of archaeology, in the light of current understandings of how and why identity groups come into being, suggests that it is very unlikely that any large-scale, named ethnic identities existed in the islands. Most people, most of the time, probably had no conscious 'ethnicity' at all beyond their own kin-group, because it was not needed. In the absence of any major external cultural Other, there was no reason to develop a sense of island-wide identity in either Britain or Ireland; indeed, as will be seen, this did not occur even when the Romans arrived. There is, then, every reason to reject a blanket, quasi-ethnic label for the peoples of either island – we should not speak of the 'Ancient Irish' or the 'Ancient Britons', let alone insular 'Celts'. Even as a general cultural description rather than an ethnic term, 'Celtic' is to be rejected because it brings an expectation of a single, universal, normative cultural model which does not fit the diverse evidence; and it also usually implies mass migrations which simply are not to be seen. Cultural similarity cannot be presumed, but must be demonstrated. Rather, we should think and speak of 'peoples of Britain and Ireland'.

THE GROWING PACE OF CHANGE: THE LATER PRE-ROMAN IRON AGE (c. 300 BC–AD 43)

From the third century BC, new patterns appear across the islands. There is a general increase in the 'visibility' of the Iron Age, with many more settlements. There was also a considerable intensification of agriculture, which expanded onto marginal land, and a more general physical dividing up of the landscape through field-systems of drainage ditches and hedgerows. All this implies production of greater disposable surplus, as does the creation of more drove-ways for movement of produce and livestock to where they were needed. As settlements in the open countryside multiplied, in many areas hillforts declined in importance: people were now living differently.

In some regions the pace of change was especially accelerated, and radically new patterns of life appear. By the time the Romans invaded in AD 43, there were very marked regional differences at a number of levels. Continental influences became considerably more evident, and the Late

Iron Age ended with southern Britain under heavy Gaulish and Roman influence, while the north and west were not.

From the third century BC, the changing face of human settlement and exploitation of the land was accompanied by a range of material innovations which also bespeak new lifestyles and new social relations. Particular attention has been given to the fine metalwork which comprises 'early Celtic art'. Examples of metalwork in late Hallstatt styles and La Tène-style 'Celtic art' have been found, the latter dating from the fourth century BC in Britain and from the third century onwards in Ireland. The objects concerned are generally similar to those seen on the continent, i.e. items of bodily adornment (such as torcs or neck-rings), weapons of war, horse and vehicle harness, sometimes feasting equipment, and items of headgear, regalia and probable religious cult items.

Some regions developed traditions of depositing such metalwork, especially in rivers and other wet environments, e.g. around the Fens (c. 300–50 BC), in northern and central Ireland (c. 250 BC to c. AD 100) and in southern Scotland (c. 100 BC to c. AD 100). These objects were evidently of great symbolic importance, but what do they signify? Generally in other parts of the isles, the last three centuries BC saw the appearance of some individual burials and small cemeteries. East Yorkshire is unique in producing large cemeteries containing hundreds of individual graves, a few richly furnished with La Tène metalwork. Such burials seem to represent a widespread new emphasis on the individual, notably the prestige of the powerful. They imply growing social differentiation, and probably the appearance of special groups or classes among many (but probably not all) of the populations of the islands. A number of features, not least La Tène metalwork with its continental flavour, also attest a new emphasis on longer-distance contacts. Could the appearance of La Tène metalwork, changes in burial practice and the appearance of foreign-style artefacts of power and war be equated with invasions? 'Celtic art' is one of the main planks in the normative model of widespread ethnic Celts across Europe. The apparent spread of such artefacts from the continent to the islands was the first material evidence taken to show 'Celtic invasions' and to fix them in the La Tène period, for the style was assumed to have arrived on the bodies of the invaders. Are these traces of the elusive 'Celts'?

What is striking about 'Celtic art' is how much of it comprises costly equipment intended for personal display, especially relating to dress, arms, equestrianism, feasting and religious ritual. It surely represents a martial, political and perhaps religious élite able to appropriate extensive economic resources. Could the appearance of this 'package' of traits perhaps represent domination of the areas where it is found by an invading continental Celtic martial élite, prefiguring the Normans? Perhaps the most striking case is that of the cemeteries of East Yorkshire, mentioned above. Here there is not the slightest doubt of strong connections with northern Gaul: both areas possess cemeteries of square-ditched burial mounds, and Yorkshire also has a few graves with La Tène weapons and/or two-wheeled vehicles, probably chariots. Is this an immigrant nobility, even an entire ethnic group? As we saw in chapter 2, the details suggest not; the graves are significantly different from those of Gaul, and the artefacts such as the pottery are in local style. The surrounding settlements also show continuity with the local past. And the La Tène artefacts in the graves are not imports, but distinctively insular versions. The Yorkshire evidence, and that from elsewhere in the isles, suggests that it was mainly ideas and ideologies – religious, socio-political, martial – that were moving, rather than people.

It is therefore suggested that some societies in some areas were generating élite groups – or perhaps the ambitious exploited the opportunity to seize military, political and religious power as populations and economic capacity expanded to make the existence of such élites viable. The appearance of La Tène finery marks the rise of *local* noble classes, and their adoption of the ideology and the lifestyle of established aristocracies in neighbouring regions, as the new nobilities sought to join the wider political and cultural circle of their peers, with whom they allied, intermarried and fought. On this view, 'Celtic art' is not a marker of ethnic identity, but of status, wealth and power, and often symbolizes specific class distinction. It would be the material part of a 'package' of ideological beliefs (such as warrior values and perhaps also religious ideas), of behaviour and ceremonial (feasting, styles of warfare, religious rites). Undoubtedly this 'package' was extensively adapted to meet local needs, as is reflected in the highly distinctive local variations of the repertoire of La Tène artefacts, styles and indeed circumstances of deposition (water offerings, cemeteries) seen across Britain and Ireland.

'Celtic art', then, is neither a mark of foreign invaders, nor evidence of general ethnic uniformity, but is a mark of *class distinction* and shared élite values across large areas which crossed ethnic boundaries. It is the mark of claimed *difference* between the self-appointed privileged and the rest of their subject peoples, through association with exclusive, exotic, foreign ways; and marks their claim to membership of a wider 'international' aristocracy. Some of those wielding such symbols may indeed have been outsiders, carving out personal power at the point of a sword (instances of 'élite domination' are apparently attested at the end of the Iron Age). However, there are highly instructive parallels from European history which support the interpretation suggested here.

Consider, for example, the case of later medieval Europe, with its many nations and peoples, yet dominated by powerful aristocracies who shared a common élite culture, of values and fashions, of power and religion, which crossed these ethnic boundaries almost effortlessly. Note also the Catholic Church of the time, with the common but locally varying material trappings of a single religious system from Portugal to Poland, and from Scotland to Sicily. Neither of these cultural phenomena are 'ethnic', and neither became established by migration or conquest from a 'core' area; wars were certainly a factor, but they mostly arose through the spread of ideas, to groups who opted to participate. Likewise, the subsequent Renaissance aristocratic culture from Madrid to Hampton Court may have found its origin in Italy, but it spread through noble and royal courts which found it suited their aspirations. But perhaps the best of all parallels for this non-ethnic interpretation of 'Celtic art' is the situation in Italy, around the same time that La Tène art arose and spread.

Italy in the sixth century BC was home to a remarkable ethnic diversity, which was more widely varied, especially in languages, than Europe north of the Alps seems to have been, ranging from Etruscans and Latins to Samnites and Greeks. Yet the noble families which ruled most of these peoples were in intimate touch with one another, fighting, intermarrying, establishing alliances, even migrating across ethnic boundaries. There was no sense of common ethnic or cultural identity in Italy until everyone became, by negotiation or conquest, Romans. For centuries these aristocracies shared common artistic styles and artefact fashions across ethnic boundaries; and these fashions found their inspiration outside, or at least on the edge of this common world – they adopted *and adapted* Greek artistic and architectural styles, aspects of religion, and social values and behaviour (such as drinking and feasting habits). Clearly, this was never an 'ethnic' process; the Italian nobilities were certainly 'Hellenized', but nobody, and least of all themselves, called them Greeks. I believe that much the same pattern prevailed across the 'Celtic' world, where a package of aristocratic values and material culture developed in one area (the zone north of the Alps) and was adopted and adapted in neighbouring regions by networks of emergent élites who found it valuable. The nature of the La Tène 'aristocratic package' was clearly very different from that of the classical Greeks; notably, La Tène élites wore, wielded and rode around in their symbolic finery, whereas Hellenized élites lived in theirs. Yet the principle is the same, and it is now quite widely accepted among archaeologists that 'Celtic art' is more about social differentiation, power and religion than about ethnicity.

Once parts of Britain and Ireland had become extensions of this wider North European network, they were not simply peripheral recipients of continental cultural trends: the islanders apparently became contributors to wider cultural developments across La Tène Europe - if Druidism really did arise in Britain and spread to the continent, as Caesar reported.

If, then, 'Celtic art' is not about ethnic identity, what group identities were articulated in Middle to Late Iron Age Britain? It is not at all clear that nobilities, petty kings and priests, whose existence implies growing scales of social organization and the plausible appearance of named political entities, were a feature seen everywhere. The people of some areas may still have had no sense of identity beyond their immediate district.

By the later Iron Age visible status divisions and religious belief systems were often much more prevalent and important dimensions of identity than vertical, ethnic divisions, and in my view this is the basic pattern behind the articulation of insular identities over the next fifteen centuries. The ethnic dimension was significant, but during that immense period of time it was exhibited at the very small scale of the many petty polities into which the islands were divided, which only very gradually began to feel any sense of wider, shared identities at all. And these expressions of ethnicity were mostly the concern of self-appointed kings and aristocracies who carved out the named polities: kings did indeed create peoples, peoples did not raise up kings. Among the mass of the population, if it meant anything at all, belonging to any named ethnic entity (especially a large 'imagined community') remained less important as a determinant of the sense of self than other dimensions, especially religion.

In such a system there will have been no need for the creation of any common self-name above those of often-transient 'tribal' groupings, because these groups did not yet have substantial contacts with other, obviously different groups with whom to contrast themselves (with the exception, perhaps, of coastal groups who were in regular contact across the Irish Sea and the Channel).

A good example of the strongly regional patterns and deep historical roots of the insular Iron Age is provided by Ireland. Hillforts and, es-

pecially in central and northern Ireland, rich 'Celtic' metalwork d
are found. But geographically the distributions of these are almost m
ally exclusive. Even more interesting is that they are separated in time
well; hillfort activity is generally centuries earlier than the metalwork
hoards and deposits, which are concentrated in the last three centuries BC
(fig. 12). This suggests differing regional traditions persisting from the
Late Bronze Age far into the Iron Age, which manifested themselves in
ways which changed greatly over time.

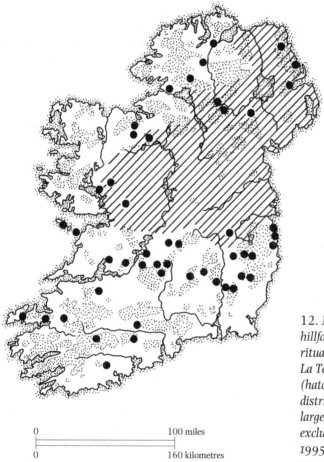

12. Map of Irish
hillforts (dots) and
ritual deposits of
La Tène metalwork
(hatched). The two
distributions are
largely mutually
exclusive (after Hill
1995 and Raftery
1994).

0   100 miles

0   160 kilometres

and also apparently underwent major social changes
the pre-Roman Iron Age, while others did not. The
of the Irish metalwork deposits after *c.* 250 BC
h the construction of the 'royal' sites of the Irish
BC. These betray little sign of continuous occupa-
l ceremonial centres later associated with mytho-
y well represent the rise of considerable social hier-
.., ..u organizing power. This, the ancestor of Cú Chulainn's world,
was an indigenous Irish development from long-term regional patterns,
not the result of foreign invasion, although it expressed itself partly
through the adoption of a version of the 'La Tène package'. Part of
Ireland was, then, involved in significant wider contacts, and may well
itself have influenced similar habits of metalwork deposition in Wales and
southern Scotland. Here is an example of a region which apparently had
stronger connections with other regions across the sea than with the rest
of the same island. Indeed, neither island seems to have been a significant
cultural unit as a whole; scales of interaction were mostly smaller, but
could straddle the seas, as Late Iron Age patterns in Britain also show.

The appearance of local élite groups implied by developments such
as these probably does mark the first manifestation of larger entities in
various regions, but these are likely to have been fiefdoms carved out by
ambitious aristocrats, superimposed onto the extant local kin-systems.
There were probably various named kingdoms, which were reliant on
personal power and generally very unstable, as the first historically attested ones – in Britain in the first century BC – certainly were, as we shall see.
How far the farming families in the countryside actually identified themselves 'ethnically' with these petty principalities we can only guess. It
seems likely that many will have felt little personal stake in such a system.
Large-scale, self-aware ethnic identities were still a thing of the future.

THE LATE IRON AGE IN THE SOUTH

In southern and eastern ('lowland') Britain the last two centuries BC saw
a continued and deepening convergence with what was happening on the
nearby continent, and a corresponding divergence with the north and
west of the archipelago, where societies continued to develop in their own
ways. However, it would be a mistake to draw too sharp a line between the
two zones. Patterns were more complex, and even in the zone of continued continental influence there is strong local diversity.

The changes across lowland Britain continued and accelerated the trends of the preceding century or two, notably in increasingly intensive settlement and exploitation of the land, and in some regions adding wholly novel dimensions to life. Ever greater numbers of objects pertaining to the body – especially, in the first century BC, vast numbers of brooches – probably indicate the further emphasis on the individual and on distinctions within societies. Regional coinages appear from the early second century BC, drawing on Gallic models, as do new pottery technologies, using a fast wheel. Up to the first century AD Kent, Essex and Hertfordshire underwent especially marked changes in settlement, ritual, material culture and social organization which made them more and more like northern France.

Julius Caesar conquered Gaul in the midst of this process, and in the account he wrote of his raids on Britain in 55 and 54 BC he gives us our first blurred historical snapshot of the social constitution of the islanders. Caesar encountered a land quite like Gaul, where parts at least of the population were divided into named units of the order of tens of thousands of people, which Caesar called *civitates*, usually translated as 'tribes' ('states' would perhaps be closer). It is a moot point how far they were real 'ethnic' units, in which most of the population accepted identity as, for example, *Trinovantes*.

These polities were ruled by powerful individuals, and there is some reason to think that they were not self-defining ethnic units, but the self-serving constructs of emergent, petty empire-building nobilities and royal dynasties who carved out and named fiefs. Caesar's most powerful antagonist, Cassivellaunus, was a warlord apparently with no named 'people' attached to him at all – although his territory north of the Thames coincides generally with that of the later powerful *Catuvellauni*. Was he a 'robber-baron' carving out a new principality as Caesar invaded? It is also striking that almost all the named 'peoples' Caesar mentions in the 50s BC had vanished a century later. This suggests great instability in these larger-scale political units, linked to the volatility of dynastic politics which remains a feature of the earliest historical records and which played a crucial role in the circumstances triggering Roman invasion.

As already mentioned, archaeology shows that the south-east was becoming intimately related to northern Gaul well before Caesar's time, and this is reflected in what he has to say about cross-Channel political dealings. Caesar records that 'within living memory' Diviciacus, ruler of the Belgic *Suessiones* (around modern Soissons), exerted power both sides of the English Channel. If he is reporting accurately, this example confirms hypotheses of both the extent and importance of dynastic kin links, and also the personal nature of power in Britain at the time. Caesar's reference to other groups of *Belgae* establishing themselves in 'the maritime districts' by military power remains enigmatic. As we have seen, most of the archaeological remains previously thought to represent these incomers are too late in date to do so. Caesar reports that identical tribal names are found in both Gaul and Britain, although he does not specify them (the names he mentions are not paralleled in Gaul). However, later in the south of Britain we do find the *Atrebates*, who share their name with a Belgic people. One of Caesar's Gallic allies, the Atrebatic prince Commius, fled to Britain, either perhaps to this related polity or maybe to establish it. In either case, this fits well with the idea that kings created 'peoples' in the later Iron Age, not the other way round: we are surely looking at a case of 'élite dominance' by military aristocrats (Britons, Gauls, or most likely an intermarried mix), not wholesale migrations.

In the decades before Caesar's raids, and increasingly thereafter, cremation burial became fashionable in parts of the south. Some tombs were especially elaborate and probably represent royalty. The luxury objects found in them – more about feasting and drinking, less about war – attest an aristocracy distinguished by wealth and privilege to a degree unprecedented in Britain, one which was effectively an extension of the system of political power on the nearby continent. The burial rites and grave-goods point up the continental connections: cremation itself, and many of the vessels interred with the dead, were Gallic imports or imitations. What we are seeing in these areas has been described as the 'Gallicization' of society. The richest graves are found near vast, straggling new settlements such as Camulodunon (Colchester) which, if not yet urban, as the analogous Gallic sites perhaps were, would often quickly become so under Roman rule. But, as with the appearance of 'Celtic art', this is very much a trend driven by the aspirations of the élites. Lowland Britain was not so much a province of Gaul, but becoming integrated into a wider political, economic and cultural zone which spanned the Channel and reached towards the Rhône Valley and the Alps (the 'Golden Banana' stretching southwards from the Thames Valley across the middle of Europe was already seen 2,000 years ago). Some graves also contain wine-jars and drinking vessels from Roman Italy: even before Caesar, a new culture of power was impinging on southern Britain.

It also seems that, decades before the Roman conquest, La Tène art was going out of use in those parts of southern Britain most in contact with Roman Gaul. Perhaps it was the loss of class cachet of La Tène-style decorated items in Gaul and Britain during the later Iron Age which led aristocrats to adopt aspects of another new, exotic, foreign cultural system, access to which they could keep exclusive; this was the Roman life-style, and initially Roman wine-drinking habits in particular, which were given enormous symbolic importance in Northern Europe.

Important though the Gallicization of the south-east is, it is another example of the strong regional differences within the islands which suggest multiple social formations of modest scale. Other areas, even neighbouring ones, followed different paths. Dorset, and the belt from Norfolk to Leicestershire, maintained strong regional characters of their own. They did not 'Gallicize', but have produced burial deposits of fine metalwork, far more than in most of the rest of the isles. If prestige objects do relate to social inequalities, these areas, too, were developing élites during the last three centuries BC, but more in their own terms than as a component of a cross-Channel system.

By the later Iron Age, some long-lasting patterns were becoming established. Increasingly, the societies of Britain were dominated by military and religious élites, which to varying degrees considered themselves as part of wider European systems of power and culture. Through sheer proximity, the south of Britain was usually the most closely integrated into continental patterns of wealth and power. Such élite domination would be typical of most insular societies until recent times, and created patterns of identity – especially ethnicity – different in kind from those of today, as aristocracies tended to seek to define larger 'ethnic' groups for their own ends, while at the same time crossing and even subverting those boundaries when personal or dynastic expediency dictated. The named 'tribal' units of the later Iron Age, then, were the especial concern, and the vehicles of power, of the aristocracies. In the context of Roman conquest, the actions of many British rulers suggest that their primary interest was personal power over their own kingdom, and as far as possible over others, rather than the collective interest of their people, let alone larger abstractions such as a sense of common 'Britishness'. Rank and religion, then, were probably more important than large ethnicities in governing life. However, it may be that the first signs of larger-scale ethnic awareness can be traced to the later Iron Age, to intense interaction with Gaul or the first encounter with Rome.

Caesar's two expeditions to Britain, in 55 and 54 BC, were near-disasters, and failed to bring the Britons under the direct rule to which the Gauls were now subjected. However, the attacks had exposed the peoples of southern Britain to a major alien power. The permanent establishment of this foreign empire just across the Channel provided them with a very different 'cultural Other' for the first time, and may have encouraged some, at least, to start consciously thinking of themselves as jointly different from Rome and from Roman Gaul – as 'Britons'. However, the subsequent story of Roman invasion suggests that this tendency was not very fully developed, and strong cultural contacts continued to be with Gallic kin and allies, through whom taste for Mediterranean ways continued to grow; while some British aristocrats, obliged by *Realpolitik* to deal with Roman imperial authority, found rapprochement with the Romans much more attractive, and more in their personal interest, than development of counter-ethnicity and resistance.

THE ROMAN IRON AGE (AD 43–*c*.410)

In AD 43, almost a century after Caesar's expeditions, the emperor Claudius dispatched a large army to establish a Roman province in Britain. The invasion was resisted fiercely – by some. Although an army raised from a number of southern peoples fought very hard in a major battle, there was no united 'national' resistance. It is clear that many regimes in Britain either welcomed the Romans openly (for reasons discussed below), or at least quickly came to terms. Yet there is a striking difference between the rapid incorporation of lowland Britain and the far slower conquest of the highland zone: it took the Romans a generation to conquer what would one day be Wales and northern England, while the future Scotland and Ireland were never to be incorporated at all (fig. 13). Hadrian's Wall was an admission of failure.

13. *Map of the islands in the middle of the Roman period, around the third century* AD. *With a few imposed modifications, the administrative map of the Roman province 'froze' and preserved the 'tribal' groupings which the Romans encountered during the conquest (*AD *40s–80s). To the north, the conformation of political groupings remained fluid; before the end of the third century, the Picts appear in the historical record. Ireland remained only vaguely understood. The names shown here are taken from Ptolemy's description of Ireland: the group names he recorded seem to be filtered through British sources. Stippled areas indicate land over 600 ft (183 m).*

CONQUERED PEOPLES

Caledones

Maeatae

Votadini

Hadrian's Wall

Carvetii

MILITARY ZONE

Parisi

Brigantes

Vennicnii
Robogdii
Darini
Erpeditani
Nagnatae
Voluntii
Eblani
Auteini
Cauci
Manapii
Gangani
Coriondi
Vellabori
Brigantes
Iverni
Usdiae

Degeangli
Cornovii
Corieltauvi
Ordovices
CIVIL PROVINCE
Iceni

Demetae
Silures
Dobunni
Catuvellauni
Trinovantes
Atrebates
Cantiaci
Belgae
Regni
Dumnonii
Durotriges

0   100 miles
0   160 kilometres

Rome's civil province of *Britannia* corresponded closely to those regions of Britain which in the later Iron Age were more or less linked into the wider Gaulish world. Pushing into the regions beyond, the Roman army ground to a halt, establishing a 'military zone' in much of Wales and northern England, leaving most of the societies around the Irish Sea beyond Roman territorial control. Such a pattern was not an accident. The limits of Roman conquest prove the continued deep diversity of societies in the islands.

There were undoubtedly some strategic factors at work in Rome's struggle to complete the conquest of the archipelago, including Ireland, which the Romans considered invading on at least one occasion. They found it much harder to operate in the more demanding terrain of Wales and the north, but it was no more impossible than the mountains of Spain, which they did subdue. Rome was also chronically distracted by other, more serious problems on other frontiers. However, a major reason for the dramatic contrast in Roman success surely lies in the contrasting social organization of the two areas. The generally smaller scale of organization, and especially the absence of the highly developed political hierarchies seen in the south, meant that these peoples were much more difficult to deal with, militarily or diplomatically. Rome was halted in Germany by similar problems: her system of assimilation, which worked well in most of Gaul and lowland Britain, did not work beyond these regions.

Lowland Britain was swiftly integrated because (like much of Gaul a century before) it already consisted of political units which corresponded quite closely to the patterns which Rome was accustomed to dealing with: substantial and productive polities already sustaining, and controlled by, clearly defined aristocracies. The Romans did not seek to destroy annexed societies; on the contrary, they sought to maintain order and harness their resources with minimum disruption. With the localized exceptions of the army (discussed below), there was no mass colonization of the new province by foreign ethnic groups. The new Roman cities, including a few military colony-cities and the port of London, apparently boasted substantial numbers of immigrants, from all over the empire (Britain's first black residents surely arrived in Roman times), but especially from Gaul and the Rhineland. Yet these amounted only to some tens of thousands in a population estimated at several million. The new province became 'Romanized' through (actually fairly selective) cultural assimilation of the indigenes. Roman practice was predicated on the existence of well-defined central aristocratic powers. It would work with friendly individual nobles or factions to control and administer conquered peoples. But societies of the highland zone of Britain generally lacked such well-defined, powerful, centralizing aristocracies with whom the Romans could negotiate.

The focus on personal political power of specific rulers is clearly visible in the establishment of Roman dominion in Britain. Before the invasion British princes, exiled in wars and coups, streamed to Rome seeking support. One of them, Verica, provided Claudius with the pretext he needed to invade. Once established, to free up troops to deal with the more difficult task of conquering upland Britain, the Romans employed a time-honoured expedient of making treaties with indigenous rulers (not with states or peoples), allowing them to govern in their own names, but in Rome's interest. A number of such 'client kings' appear to have struck such bargains, notably Prasutagus of the *Iceni* (on whose death, Roman mismanagement of the incorporation of the *Iceni* into the province triggered the terrible Boudican revolt). It seems that the 'kingdoms' established for such favoured aristocrats need not correspond at all to the pre-conquest map of polities: for example, the kingdom of the man taken to be Verica's successor, Togidubnus (or Cogidubnus), that of the *Regni*, seems to have been carved out of southern Britain by Roman fiat, as apparently was another new *civitas*, that of the *Belgae*. The map of the province, like that of the later Iron Age, was essentially created by, or for, powerful nobles, rather than reflecting voluntary 'ethnic' associations by the mass of the people.

A key reason why imperial rule was accepted, and probably welcomed, by many nobles was that rapprochement with Rome stabilized and guaranteed their local power with the backing of Roman military force. The empire secured favoured aristocrats against enemies among their peers and against their social inferiors. Clear advantage lay with co-operation: they were quite happy to adopt Roman ways and to become Roman citizens through supporting the imperial power. 'Tribal' ethnicity, and any nascent sense of British identity, if it yet existed at all, was evidently much weaker than dynastic self-interest. They were not 'unpatriotic': patriotism as we understand it, and mass emotional identification with a national or ethnic ideal are phenomena of a much later and utterly different world. However, the mass uprising of the *Iceni* and their neighbours under Boudica shows that common ethnic and apparently religious feeling could be stirred up in the face of an alien Other.

The named Iron Age 'peoples' such as the *Atrebates*, *Catuvellauni* and *Corieltauvi* became fossilized as the administrative cantons of the Roman province. If there had ever been mass adherence to these identities during the later Iron Age, it is likely to have become much attenuated under Roman rule, which banned the regional conflicts which may have given Iron Age ethnic distinctions some edge. Under the Romans wealth and class divisions, even further exaggerated than in the Late Iron Age, became the most important dimension of social division.

The army, as a centre of clear Roman political and cultural identity in Britain, is an especially fascinating case, since it was initially composed of soldiers from all over the Roman empire, from as far away as Spain, North Africa, Bulgaria and Syria. These were welded together, by the end of the second century AD, into a virtual military caste of men who held Roman citizenship, a body which was largely hereditary and which topped up its ranks from the province in which it was stationed. Britain long had a large garrison of around 50,000 men which, in a province of perhaps three million people, had an influence out of all proportion to its numbers, due to its political power and economic demands. In the early years a handful of military *coloniae* were implanted to supplement security and provide for veterans, but again the numbers involved were only some thousands. The soldiers, concentrated in the military zone beyond the civil province, represented the largest body of ethnic incomers to the island.

Stretching across the middle of Britain, from Wales to the Pennines and sometimes extending to the Forth/Clyde line, the military zone of Roman Britain had a unique character, that of two societies which largely turned their backs on each other. Mostly Roman citizens, the soldiers, with their attendant civilian communities, were in a way the most Roman part of Britain, linked directly as they were to the Roman military communities of other provinces. But the populations amongst which most of the soldiers were garrisoned seem to have been at least passively resistant to Roman culture; typically their farmsteads show little sign of an interest in Roman tastes. It may be that the more bloodily fought conquest in these areas had largely destroyed the indigenous military élites, or, as in the Scottish Highlands after1745, permanently prevented them pursuing the traditional lifestyle on which the existing social order depended. The Roman army itself surely fulfilled the role of a dominating martial élite in these regions, one which was culturally quite separate from the bulk of the population. As in the heart of the civil province, it is not at all clear how far the mass of the rural population regarded their own ethnic status, but the pre-Roman 'tribal' units did not survive the occupation.

As we have seen, the Romans did not even regard the Britons as all the same, but distinguished between *Britanni* in the south and *Brittones* in the North. We do not know whether these were Roman labels or 'ethnic' self-names of groupings of British peoples. Nor do we know exactly what the distinction was or where the boundary lay, but it is significant that the Romans did regard Britain as consisting of two different zones. However, it is clear that the imperial presence certainly did see, perhaps for the first time, large numbers of people in the island identifying themselves ethnically as part of a much larger 'imagined community': that of 'the Romans'. To many, such as soldiers of provincial origin (recruited from elsewhere or, later, from Britain itself), and local British notables who were granted citizenship, being Roman may have been an additional level of identity. But, as we shall see, the association of 'Roman-ness' with increasingly untrammelled power and privilege makes it unlikely that the bulk of the provincial population became enthusiastic Romans, even when they acquired citizenship, as almost all did by AD 212.

Paradoxically, the eruption of this alien power into the archipelago may also have encouraged the development of the first large-scale *indigenous* ethnic identities – among those the Romans sought, but failed, to incorporate.

BEYOND THE PROVINCE

The Roman advance to the north and west ground to a halt in the Scottish Borders, and despite campaigns as far as the Moray Firth and intermittent occupation up to modern Glasgow and Edinburgh, the limits of permanent direct rule were really marked by Hadrian's Wall. However, Roman hegemony certainly reached far beyond this line. Through military and diplomatic intervention, through trade, and later as a target for attack, the brooding presence of the empire so nearby certainly had important effects on 'Free Caledonia' and Ireland.

Proximity to Roman imperial power and to the developed province did affect the unconquered lands. Roman military threats and political interference probably helped to precipitate the first larger political agglomerations in northernmost Britain. By the fourth century AD, a substantial new power, the Picts (as they were called by Roman writers), existed to the north of the province. A heterogeneous group of Caledonian 'tribes' coalesced into a well-defined kingdom, which was to outlast Roman power by several centuries. The Picts arose in what appears to be a classic environment of contact with a threatening cultural Other against which common interests and values might be defined and new identities forged. They may have possessed a more fully developed sense of ethnic identity, more widely shared across the social spectrum, than had been the case with the aristocratic polities of the Late Iron Age south, which were arising before Rome appeared on the scene. Although important, the Picts were only part of the picture; the future Scotland was still a region of multiple identities.

Whether proximity to Roman power also encouraged the beginnings of a sense of shared and distinctive Irishness is unclear. Ireland during the Roman period is still a land almost unknown to history. Insulated as it was from the direct attentions of Roman imperialism by the Irish Sea (although diplomatic contacts are to be expected, and trading and aristocratic contacts with Roman Britain are detectable archaeologically), it seems unlikely that the presence of Rome at such a remove would have precipitated a strong, island-wide sense of identity, any more than the similar situation of Britain had between Caesar and Claudius. For centuries to come, regional distinctions within the island continued to be much more important. This was broadly the period looked back to by the surviving Irish myths such as the adventures of Cú Chulainn, which focus on the conflicts between the large, provincial 'super-kingdoms' such as Ulster and Connacht, but the origins and integrity of these tales remain obscure. Long after the collapse of Roman power, Ireland remained a shifting patchwork of very small sub-kingdoms with an unstable hierarchy of larger provincial overlordships. The historical role of the famous site of Tara remains enigmatic, the idea of effective 'high kingship of all Ireland' at the time essentially a myth. How far the people in the countryside even voluntarily identified themselves as subjects of the various petty kings is unknown, for their voices are not heard.

During the last decades of Roman power in Britain, groups from Ireland joined the many other 'barbarians' in exploiting the growing weakness of the empire. They raided the western coasts of Britain, and in places started to settle. They were known to the Romans and Romano-British as *Scotti*. The details show that these attacks were a matter of private enterprise by individuals and small kingdoms, including the raiding which, early in the fifth century, took the young St Patrick to Ireland as a slave. As we shall see in the case of Irish settlement in western Scotland, much of this activity was an extension of Irish dynastic power politics onto a larger stage.

The warlike maritime activities of the *Scotti* were matched in the North

Sea by Saxons and other 'pirates' from the continent. Eastern Britain was starting to be part of an expanded field of contact and conflict now including Germany and Scandinavia as well as Roman Europe, a North Sea world which would henceforth be vital to its history.

THE END OF ROMAN BRITAIN

Lowland Britain was famously changed by Roman power, dotted with towns, criss-crossed with paved roads, and, eventually, scattered with masonry villas, some of them palatial. All this represents the establishment of Roman provincial culture in Britain. Further, Roman citizenship spread rapidly, initially among the privileged, who are seen as the builders of the towns and villas. But from the early third century almost the whole population was granted Roman citizenship. Legally speaking at least, lowland Britons, rich and poor, were now generally Roman citizens. But how did they see themselves? Even in the Roman period, there is an acute shortage of documentary sources, even for the rich of this peripheral province: the rural masses remain 'peoples without history', pretty much as their Iron Age ancestors had been. To address these questions we are still heavily reliant on archaeology and on inference from the better historical evidence of neighbouring provinces.

Most of the Romanization of the province was associated with the powerful, or with outsiders: the army and provincial administration, traders moving between the cities and across the Channel, and, in the provincial towns and the countryside, the 'Romanized' indigenous aristocracies. Away from the towns and villas, what is striking is the relative *lack* of impact that incorporation into the Roman world had on the mass of farming families.

The coming of Rome did not revolutionize agriculture. For a long time people lived the same lifestyle and pursued the same established and effective farming regimes as before the conquest. Much of the population continued to live in round houses, not square Romanized ones. It is mainly the presence of pots and brooches in Roman style and imperial coins (needed to pay taxes) that tells us we are in Roman times and not the Iron Age. Romanization was primarily the concern of the powerful: citizenship and Roman taste were the new ways in which the privileged could mark themselves out as inherently different from the poor, just as possession of La Tène finery and then adoption of Gallic lifestyles and Italian wine-drinking had marked them out in earlier times. By the third century, as citizenship spread to the poor (largely to extend the tax base), life gradually changed in the countryside, and by the end of Roman times the ancient tradition of round architecture had given way to the rectangular tradition we still have today. But significantly, the gap between the 'haves' and the 'have-nots' was still widening. The fourth century was the period of a few truly splendid, palatial villas, and the time when many more modest ones at last got baths, hypocausts and mosaics. But these still represented only a tiny percentage of the population: at the same time the majority, although citizens, were losing rights due to changes in Roman law, which now formally distinguished between privileged *honestiores* and the increasingly oppressed *humiliores*. In better-documented areas such as Gaul, many peasants were tied to the land, prefiguring medieval serfdom, and distress led to widespread peasant revolts. Were things the same in Roman Britain?

It can be argued that Rome's relatively successful civil province in Britain was actually the continuation, and development 'under new management', of the pre-existing cross-Channel region of interaction seen in the later Iron Age. It saw a deepening of the distinctions between base and noble which were growing progressively in southern Britain from the third century BC. Increasing identification of the provincial aristocracies with Roman imperial power resulted in further decline of traditional links of mutual obligation between nobles and peasantry, the kind of alienation and social dislocation seen in the Scottish Highlands after the 1745 Rising. In such an extremely class-divided, indeed class-polarized society, it might be suggested that the cultural values and identity so ostentatiously displayed by the ruling class, in their opulent villas (albeit mostly pale imitations of Gallic or Italian ones), their mosaics and baths and splendid silver table services, might be looked on with little enthusiasm by the mass of the rural population who paid for them. Was the long-lasting cultural conservatism of the peasantry due to exclusion by their superiors from Roman-style life? Or did it represent cultural resistance to the dominant powers, both imperial and native-aristocratic?

Late Roman times saw an imperial administration in league with aristocratic landowners to squeeze rents and taxes from the peasantry, their authority guaranteed by the army. All these groups undoubtedly regarded themselves as fully Roman in their primary identity. How did the rural peasantry see themselves? The subsequent dramatic fate of the province seems to me to suggest that they were not much enamoured of their social superiors, or of the dubious privilege of being Roman. This probably helps to explain the rapid collapse of Roman lifestyle and ethnic identity in Britain in the fifth century.

THE EARLY MEDIEVAL PERIOD

(*c*.AD 400–*c*.1100)

In AD 400, the southern half of Britain was still part of the Roman empire, while the north and Ireland were patchworks of 'barbarian' kingdoms. By AD 1100, the map of the isles was substantially as we see it in modern times, especially in Britain, where the three familiar nations had appeared in roughly the territories we still know. This represents a dramatic shift, not least in the replacement of Celtic- and Latin-speaking Romano-British society by Germanic-speaking England. This has long been explained in terms of Anglo-Saxon invasions and migrations, destroying or displacing westwards the Romano-British. Is this really what happened?

The 'fire and sword' image which still widely prevails, of Roman Britain going down under the onslaught of massive Germanic Anglo-Saxon military invasion, is as suspect as the alleged Celtic invasions of a thousand years earlier. With a few exceptions, excavation of large numbers of Romano-British sites, from towns to forts, villas and farms almost always reveals gradual dilapidation, or careful demolition and abandonment, or so-called 'squatter' occupation. Sometimes there is subsequent 'Anglo-Saxon' occupation on or near the site. It now looks as though the 'Germanic invasions', like the 'Celtic' ones, are the result of retrospective recasting of the past to suit the needs of later generations, starting in later Anglo-Saxon times and further modified since. Much of the problem arises from over-literal reading of early sources such as the British monk Gildas, who was writing not history as we understand it, but religious polemic, full of apocalyptic biblical allegory.

Although the traditional history we have inherited is based on real wars in the post-Roman centuries, these were generally small in scale, and less catastrophic than they were described. It was a story that fitted the needs of military aristocracies and royal houses which were now part of the North Sea world and which had a requirement for suitably heroic foundation myths and an ideological base for what was happening in the eighth to tenth centuries – the consolidation of Anglo-Saxon power and identity, at least among the ruling classes. Bede's famous characterization of the settlement of continental Angles, Saxons and Jutes now seems also to be more about the politics of the eighth century than the realities of the fifth and sixth. The corresponding classes of warriors and rulers among the northern and western peoples, not least those whose descendants would one day be Welsh, were equally preoccupied with war and power, and this is reflected in the surviving literature, in poems such as *The Gododdin*.

Roman Britain's fate was less apocalyptic than usually thought, but perhaps more puzzling. Imperial power in Britain certainly collapsed in the early decades of the fifth century, and Romanized life, culture and identity in the lowland zone apparently vanished with astonishing speed and totality. The precise chronology is hard to establish, because of the sparseness of contemporary accounts and because almost all archaeological dating indicators cease. The province ceased to be an effective part of the empire by AD 410, and maintenance of villas, towns and forts also ceased during the first decade or two of the century. It is interesting to note that much of this decline had been in progress for some decades (examples being the contraction of the pottery industry and a reduction in building on villa sites): the prominent manifestations of Roman economy and life-style were already faltering well before the end of imperial rule.

What caused this speedy and thorough collapse? This pattern was not generally seen in other provinces overrun by 'barbarians' when the Western Empire fell in the fifth century. Elsewhere, Roman law and administration and the Church (Christianity became Rome's official religion in the fourth century) all continued. It is now apparent that the 'Fall of the West' really comprised the extinction of the imperial regime and the Roman army. Roman life generally survived, under new, immigrant Germanic nobilities, such as the Visigoths in Spain, the Franks in Gaul and the Ostrogoths in Italy itself. These invaders did not want to destroy Roman life but to benefit from it, so they protected, and generally integrated with, the existing provincial aristocracies and ecclesiastical powers. Syntheses of Roman and 'barbarian' culture transformed the old provinces into medieval continental Europe which, west of the Rhine, has mostly spoken Latin-derived Romance tongues ever since.

What was different about Roman Britain, especially as it was insulated by the seas from the sudden, massive incursions of warriors and even whole populations which apparently afflicted Gaul? On New Year's Eve 406/7 the Rhine froze, and vast numbers of Germans poured into Gaul, intending to settle. But if these huge numbers did not destroy Roman life in Gaul, why did it disappear so completely in Britain? The mystery apparently deepens when it is realized that there is very little evidence for 'fire and sword' being responsible for the collapse of the province. The story of the middle decades of the fifth century is not one of substantial foreign incursions but of . . . nothing. Or so it seems.

A lack of datable artefacts makes it hard to chart this almost ahistorical period archaeologically, but environmental evidence shows that farming continued: there was no total demographic collapse due to plague or the flight of the rural population. People were there, but currently we cannot 'see' them archaeologically. The meagre documentary sources of the period suggest that 'Germanic' military power, in the form of immigrant mercenary war-bands, began to make itself felt only around the middle of the fifth century, according to the traditional document-based chronology; currently the archaeological dating for the appearance of North-Sea-style cultural remains, traditionally equated with Anglo-Saxon invaders, is hotly contested. Roman Britain seems to have collapsed up to half a century before the new, alien 'Germanic' tradition made much impact.

Roman culture and identity in lowland Britain was not directly destroyed by the Anglo-Saxons; paradoxically its fall was probably an indirect result of the incursions of the Franks and others into Gaul in 406–7, cutting Britain off from the central empire. The province could no longer call on additional military support. Loss of support from the army left the power and authority of the provincial administration and of the rich ruling class or landowners highly vulnerable – especially when this regime could no longer even pretend to be defending the population. Without recourse to the central imperial power, the provincial élite had no means of maintaining its authority; perhaps many nobles simply could no longer enforce their will in extracting rents and taxes. There may have been open peasant revolts, as there were on a massive scale in Gaul. The ensuing collapse of the Romanized ruling superstructure left a peasantry which had neither the means, nor probably much desire, to be Roman. The last traces of pre-Roman social order had been transformed out of recognition under Roman rule, and in Britain vanished with the villa-dwelling landlords before the Anglo-Saxons became a power on the scene. When groups from across the North Sea really began to make their presence felt in the latter part of the fifth century, they moved into a vacuum – not a depopulated wilderness, but a land where people had lost, or perhaps rejected, their former cultural identity. Nominally Roman, the population on the land probably had little clear sense of common ethnic identity, beyond their local communities.

The late fifth and sixth centuries saw the appearance in the landscape of cemeteries with alien rites and new types of artefacts – a material culture which clearly relates to that of the continent, from north-west Germany to Sweden. Traditionally, these have been seen as the remains of the hordes of invading Angles, Saxons and Jutes, who seized the lands of future England by killing the benighted Britons or driving them west into nascent Wales, Cornwall and Brittany. Undoubtedly there was warfare, and there were refugees, but it is evident that in many areas of eastern Britain large enclaves of indigenous peoples survived, some as autonomous petty kingdoms. Some of the 'Anglo-Saxon' states, such as Northumbria, were apparently populated very largely by Britons, with relatively few immigrants. It now seems certain that in the lands which, during the sixth century, began to crystallize into a patchwork of 'Anglo-Saxon' kingdoms, much, even most, of the population was of indigenous origin. Currently, some medieval archaeologists would go further, in questioning how far the 'Anglo-Saxon' cemeteries and settlement sites represent immigrants at all, rather than the cultural transformation of indigenous British communities.

It is clear that, after the end of Roman rule, eastern Britain soon became a full part of the North Sea zone. Instead of a massive one-way flow of new people from the continent to Britain, the situation may have been a good deal more reciprocal, with individuals and groups crossing and recrossing the seas in all directions. As in the Late Iron Age, when southern Britain shared the culture of nearby Gaul, and as in the Roman period, when it was the most fully assimilated into provincial culture, so now eastern Britain partook of the dominant 'Germanic' culture of the North Sea region, adopting and sharing in the material trappings and the dialects through which power was expressed. Eastern Britain came to look 'Germanic' only partly because it was settled by newcomers from across the sea. Since Roman ways were no longer available, and (it is suggested) in this region no longer carried prestige anyway, indigenous people of the region who sought status in society were obliged to express it in terms of the new dominant tradition: and so eastern Britons 'Germanized'. A hitherto little appreciated, underlying continuity from Romano-British times is now becoming visible in aspects of 'Anglo-Saxon' culture. For example, study of butchery practices shows they are drawn from insular, not continental traditions, and although the fine timber halls of the sixth and seventh centuries found across much of eastern Britain relate to continental long-houses in external appearance, the ground-plans of many are identical in size and layout to late Romano-British dwellings. Further, some forms of artefacts such as particular 'Anglo-Saxon' brooch types are actually insular inventions. As with La Tène art, Anglo-Saxon artefacts are more often local variations on a common theme than foreign imports.

All this was retrospectively rewritten, notably by Bede, into a much more purposeful and directed invasion by specific peoples, with far more clear-cut results than was actually the case. The Anglo-Saxon kingdoms were created from the top down by ambitious warlords, and were legitimized by refiguring the past into clearer heroic histories with roots across the North Sea. Whatever their actual ethnic origins – and Cerdic, credited founder of the West Saxon royal house, had a British, not German name – their membership of the North Sea and Baltic world is expressed wonderfully in the poem *Beowulf* and in the Swedish connections of many of the objects in the grave of an East Anglian king at Sutton Hoo.

If, as in the Late Iron Age, kings made peoples in post-Roman lowland Britain, and if the population consisted of descendants of the Romano-British who had lost or rejected Roman identity, mixed with unknown but highly varied proportions of people from the continent who largely arrived as small communities to settle, rather than as great tribes of conquerors, what was the ethnic map like in, say, AD 550? Identities were surely in tremendous flux, and the superstructure of nominal kingdoms such as Wessex and Mercia probably became once again primarily the concern of the ambitious and powerful. Notions of English ethnicity only began to arise much later.

THE INDIGENOUS KINGDOMS AFTER ROME

In northern Britain, the long-established Pictish kingdom was a major power. It faced two alien presences: 'Germanic' Northumbria to the south, and settlers from Ireland in the west. Between Hadrian's Wall and the Forth/Clyde line, a similar pattern prevailed. A group of small kingdoms arose; the *Votadini* in Lothian became the Gododdin, while those in the west formed the kingdoms of Strathclyde and Rheged.

To match the developing 'Germanic' states of the east, during the post-Roman centuries a patchwork of small British-speaking kingdoms arose from the fragments of the rest of the old Roman province from Cornwall to Cumbria, joining those which already existed beyond the old frontier. Although often under military pressure from the east and from Ireland, some showed considerable aggression of their own: western Britons took control of Armorica in Gaul, causing havoc as far as the Loire and establishing what became the kingdom of Brittany.

In those areas of western Britain that would one day be Cumbria, Wales and Cornwall, Roman rule had not transformed indigenous societies as radically as in the south and east. Emerging again as many small kingdoms, they were internally unstable and prone to complete collapse, fission or fusion, like the proto-states of the Late Iron Age south. They quickly regenerated martial élites, which clearly perceived the newcomers in the east as 'barbarians' with whom they were soon fighting. Shared ethnic identity as Britons was perhaps sharpened by contrast with this perceived new alien Other, and with a second, the Irish *Scotti*, raiding and settling the western coasts. A major focus of perceived difference between the British peoples and their enemies was religion as much as wider ethnic traits: the Britons were largely Christian, the 'Anglo-Saxons' and initially the *Scotti* were pagans. Such is the context of Arthur, if he was historical – no king, but a joint war-leader like Cassivellaunus, Caratacus, Boudica and Calgacus before him.

The impact of the *Scotti* was most lasting in the north. A branch of the Dál Riata (Dalriada) dynasty from nearby Antrim in Ireland established itself in Argyll, apparently due to dynastic pressures at home. How far there was substantial colonization from Ireland is unclear, but the Western Highlands were essentially Irish-speaking (Gaelic, 'Erse') from this period onwards, if not earlier (there were clearly very long-standing and close connections between north-east Ireland and adjacent areas of Scotland).

What about self-identity in Ireland itself? Did a sense of common Irishness exist when some groups were happily raiding and settling in Britain? It seems likely that at most regional identities, or even dynastic ones, predominated, again perhaps more the concern of self-serving élites than of the farming families on whom they relied. The Irish footholds in Britain such as Dál Riata were the affairs of particular dynasties, not 'peoples'. It will be suggested that a common, self-aware Irish identity really began to develop only later, when Viking raids and settlement presented the first direct threat of an entirely alien people on Irish soil.

POWER, RELIGION AND ETHNICITY IN
THE EARLY MEDIEVAL PERIOD

The post-Roman centuries may have seen the more widespread establishment of lasting ethnic identities, which had begun with the intrusive presence of Rome and continued with the larger-scale, longer-distance conflicts between more obviously different groups, for example with the presence of Irish and continental warrior groups in Britain, and later with Vikings in both islands. But these identities did not line up simply along the axis of 'Celt' and 'German': Britons were often in conflict with the Irish as well as with Anglo-Saxon kingdoms.

Religion, probably more than any other cultural dimension, was important in determining group boundaries in the post-Roman centuries. The distinctions between Britons and *Scotti*, and between British and 'Anglo-Saxon' polities ('Anglo-Saxon' was itself a term yet to be coined), were initially expressed particularly in terms of Christian and pagan. Once Christianity became general in the seventh century, differences between the indigenous British and Irish Churches and the Roman Church became significant for a while, but Christianity also became an axis of communication and political linkage between the various developing identities which transcended and subverted any ethnic boundaries. For example, the Anglian nobility of Northumbria had especially strong connections with the Pictish kingdom and with Dál Riata, and these 'diplomatic relations' were largely articulated through ecclesiastical connections (and prominent priests were themselves often aristocrats, like St Columba). King Oswiu spent his exile on Iona, and Irish churchmen were central to the flourishing of the great Northumbrian monastic centres, forming channels through which the insular cultures influenced each other more generally, across 'ethnic' boundaries. Irish and Irish-trained Anglo-Saxon scholars and evangelists from this common ecclesiastical world were tremendously influential across continental Europe.

Dynastic and especially religious connections, then, were often much more important than ethnic or general cultural differences between privileged, politically active groups. If the existence of named group identities like the multitude of early medieval kingdoms was only one of several factors concerning the powerful, and these kingdoms were highly volatile and unstable, were there any large-scale, clearly defined ethnicities as such in the islands? The engagement of the bulk of the population in such affairs was probably still minimal, especially away from centres of power or contested border zones.

THE VIKINGS: CATALYSTS OF ETHNOGENESIS?

In 793 the first Viking raid struck Lindisfarne in Northumbria, and the Norse were attacking Ireland before the century was out. A mix of Danes and Norwegians, these prodigious mariners, traders and colonizers have been remembered primarily as ferocious raiders, in which guise, during the ninth century in particular, they changed the political map of the islands (fig. 14).

Viking attacks, and increasing settlement, imperilled all the many kingdoms of the archipelago to an almost unprecedented degree. Ireland had never faced such a sustained attack by alien people; they caused widespread terror and disruption, although, unlike in Britain, the political and cultural order was never seriously endangered. Across the Irish Sea, the very existence of whole kingdoms was at stake, and indeed several Anglo-Saxon royal houses were wiped out. The military threat was demonstrably grave, but it is notable that, once again, it was religious difference which received most attention: for the Northmen, rapacious alien Others, were above all characterized as pagans.

It is no accident that this period saw the formation of the three nations of Britain which are with us still: the unpredictability and ferocity of the Viking assaults – exemplified in the horrific martyrdoms of several Anglo-

14. *The archipelago around the ninth and tenth century* AD, *during which period Viking armies ranged over much of Britain and Ireland and many areas were subject to substantial Norwegian and Danish settlement. These activities helped to precipitate the unification of the kingdoms of the Picts and Dál Riata into the new kingdom of Scotland. The disruption of the multiple Anglo-Saxon kingdoms in eastern Britain also culminated in the appearance of a unified English state. The map is greatly simplified, and cannot convey the complexity of either British or Irish dynastic politics during the period. Stippled areas indicate land over 600 ft (183 m).*

 Main areas of Norwegian Viking settlement

 Main areas of Danish Viking settlement

[Picts]

ALBA
(Scotland)

Strathclyde

Northumbria

[Dál Riata]

Cóiced Ulad

Cóiced Connacht

Mide

Cóiced Laigen

Cóiced Muman

Gwynedd

Powys

Offa's Dyke

Mercia

East Angles

Deheubarth

Morgannwg

ANGLO-SAXON
KINGDOMS

West Saxons

Cornwall

0   100 miles

0   160 kilometres

117

Saxon kings – constitute the kind of environment which one might expect to foster mass engagement in ethnogenesis.

The unified Scottish and English kingdoms were both established in the context of fierce pressure from the Vikings, and the consolidation of their national identities came in the aftermath. Although both unifications were largely dynastic in political terms, the sense of common peril from the alien outsiders perceived by kings, nobles and commoners alike in each kingdom was probably vital in creating widespread consent and support for the new states. The appearance of unitary Scottish and English states represented the culmination of long-term processes of negotiation and conflict between the constituent kingdoms, and might have occurred eventually anyway, but it seems likely that the essential catalyst which precipitated their integration, and which helped give them their initial shape and cohesion, was the alien presence, and tangible threat, of the Vikings as raiders and settlers.

In the case of Scotland, during the ninth century both Dál Riata and the Picts faced serious dangers from the Vikings, who disrupted the former's vital communications with Ireland and who were seizing Pictish-controlled territory. This was the context of the final political union of the two kingdoms, followed by more profound cultural integration during the tenth century. Under the new, chosen name of *Alba* (Scotland), the Pictish and Gaelic groups of the kingdom began for the first time to think of themselves as one, in a hybrid polity which retained many aspects of Pictish social structure but with Gaelic language and culture dominant (the Pictish language vanished, along with much Pictish culture and history, apparently deliberately suppressed). Early Scotland was mainly the Pictish state transformed; the old territorial centre of Dál Riata was lost to the Vikings.

Once established, the more powerful Scotland grew by accretion of ethnically diverse groups, absorbing the Anglian populations south of the Forth, and the British kingdom of Strathclyde in the eleventh century. As Viking power waned, so Scotland's expansion brought it into increasing contact with another major new kingdom: England.

To the south, the various Anglo-Saxon kingdoms had contended for power with one another as much as with the British realms. Northumbria and Mercia in particular had been dominant. Norse attacks, and increasing settlement in the east, completely disrupted this pattern. Viking destruction of the royal houses of several Anglo-Saxon kingdoms actually helped clear the political stage for unification of England under the

West Saxon royal house, when the latter was finally able to defeat the Norse in the early tenth century. The largely Danish military conquest and partial settlement of the northern and eastern Anglo-Saxon areas added a new ethnic component to the map, but paradoxically the formerly feared Scandinavians rapidly integrated, politically and to a large degree culturally, especially once they settled and converted to Christianity, removing a major source of cultural conflict. Integration was perhaps fairly easy, since both indigenes and newcomers shared membership of the North Sea world, and Viking York in particular was a major centre of long-distance trade and cultural contact. Eleventh-century England was ruled by squabbling dynasties of English and Scandinavian aristocrats and kings, until its conquest by the Normans (in origin another group of Viking warlords).

Wales, too, emerges as a single political entity about the same period. Early cultural identity among the western Britons drew on the traditions of the indigenous peoples of Cumbria and the Scottish borders as well as the future Wales (as in the North British poem *The Gododdin*), but recognizably Welsh identity was actually formed in the context of the mountainous peninsula to which growing Anglo-Saxon power confined it, physically defined by Offa's Dyke. Mercia provided the principal cultural Other for the ethnogenesis of the Welsh, although the Irish, and later the Vikings, also played significant roles. The ethnonym which they adopted, *Cymry*, originally meant simply 'the people'; 'Welsh' was an English term meaning 'foreigner'. From the several petty kingdoms of the peninsula a unified Welsh kingdom arose in the ninth century, under Rhodri Mawr (the Great), forged in the face of war with the Vikings and English. Although politically it was initially an aristocratic construct, Wales was developing an identifiable common culture as well, reflected in the single Welsh law code promulgated by Rhodri's grandson Hywel Dda (the Good).

From the 830s Viking assaults on Ireland intensified, and they started to settle – Dublin was their most important foundation. While they also constituted an alarming cultural Other in Ireland, the Vikings caused less structural damage to the existing order there than in Britain. For instance, they did not overthrow the existing pattern of kingship, but joined in Irish dynastic politics as additional 'players'. The death in battle against them of Brian Boru at Clontarf in 1014 did not mark the defeat of a looming Norse conquest, but was a failed attempt to establish real high kingship over Ireland, which remained a network of competing powers thereafter.

Nevertheless, exposure to the depredations of these foreign pagans probably marked a significant step in the development of a shared Irish ethnic consciousness.

In all these squabbling kingdoms, power was concentrated in the hands of aristocracies, among whom issues of group-names and identities were a central concern. It remains difficult to assess how far the people at large, farming and stock-raising across Britain and Ireland, actively identified with such regimes – especially as borders shifted, overlords killed one another, and new powers emerged on the ruins of vanished ones. We can expect a wide variation in response, according to circumstances. A sense of solidarity across society which may be called ethnic was most likely to develop where there was a common perceived threat from apparently very different groups – such as the Vikings.

That entities called England, Scotland and Wales should have arisen from the complex patchwork of cultures and politics in Britain from the ninth century onwards was not inevitable, but is an example of the importance of historical contingency. While Norse power encouraged groupings to draw together, the pattern of Viking domination was instrumental in constraining how this would come about, especially in cutting off from each other the Pictish world and the southern Anglo-Saxons. By the time nascent England incorporated the intervening Viking territories, a substantial new Scottish entity already existed, with an increasingly distinctive culture and separate Church. Without the Vikings, some quite different pattern of power and identity would have arisen.

Indeed, until the Viking period the cultural and political patterns of early medieval Britain echoed those of the pre-Roman centuries more than they prefigured the modern world. While the lands bordering the western seas, from Brittany to the Hebrides, looked more towards each other than to the east, lowland Britain looked towards France and the Rhine as much as to the west for its political and cultural connections. Indeed, at times the south and east, and especially Kent, were virtually part of the Frankish hegemonic world. Across the islands, deep into the second millennium AD, while a general sense of belonging to the larger political entity was surely growing, regional identities remained the most important for most of the people (especially the rural poor), most of the time.

THE LATER MEDIEVAL PERIOD

(c.1100–c.1500)

Larger and more destructive conflicts between the nations of Britain and nearby continental Europe, arising especially from royal ambitions, caused the development of more clearly defined ethnic/national identities during the thirteenth to fifteenth centuries.

By the time of the Norman invasion of England in 1066, Britain consisted of the three kingdoms we still know. Yet how far these represented unified ethnic entities is not clear. Did farmers and villagers feel themselves to be 'English' or 'Scottish', especially when, a few generations before, they had been Mercians or Danes, or subjects of the Kingdom of Strathclyde? Was there a greater sense of ethnic consciousness shared between base and noble in Wales, which was forged under more drastic foreign cultural pressure? Even here there were (and still are) very strong differences between north and south.

Ethnic identities in Ireland and Britain during the later Middle Ages were largely forged through the consequences of attempts by Norman French kings to build an English-based empire in the archipelago. The repeated devastation caused by this partially successful enterprise further sharpened the determination of the colonized to be something other than English, at a time when, somewhat ironically, English speech and ethnicity constituted a subordinate culture in its own land.

The Norman conquest of England eliminated Anglo-Saxon social leaders and replaced them with a French-speaking military colonial élite. This marked direct extension into England of the politically ascendant aristocratic culture of France and neighbouring regions. The English-speaking majority formed a highly regionalized ethnic underclass, in which 'Englishness' was not clearly defined and which under Norman rule could not find an easy means of expression. From the eleventh to the fourteenth centuries, England possessed a complex, two-tier, class-based ethnic structure.

The wars prosecuted by the increasingly powerful kings of England, however, especially from the thirteenth to the fifteenth centuries, were responsible for the development and consolidation of the insular national identities we still know. The Welsh and Scots created their sense of identity in opposition to Anglo-Norman power.

In the twelfth century, the peoples of Scotland, plural, were even more diverse than before, now incorporating Norman French and Flemish settlers, but all came together under the Scottish royal banner to fight the English, as at the Battle of the Standard in 1138. Increasingly determined attempts, especially by Edward I, to annexe Scotland led to the Wars of Independence personified by William Wallace and Robert the Bruce. The wars forged a growing national consciousness among the ethnically diverse nobility, expressed not least in the importance attached to a separate Scottish Church, determined not to be subject to York and Canterbury. These developments are seen in a significant shift in attitudes among Scots nobles around 1300; before that, they accepted that the King of the Scots had the right to accept English overlordship, if he deemed it appropriate. But the 1320 Declaration of Arbroath expresses an important ideological change, in that the community of Scots was deemed to have an inalienable right to independent existence, to which the King's wishes were subordinate.

Yet Scotland also remained internally complex. The Northern Isles were a Norwegian possession until the late Middle Ages, and are still culturally distinct. And as Lowland Scotland and the royal court became more integrated into wider Europe, so around 1400 a division opened up with Highland Scottish culture which lasted until the eighteenth century.

Edward I was more successful in Wales. Welsh high kingship had been destroyed by Norman power before the end of the eleventh century. Llywelyn Fawr (the Great), last Prince of Wales, was killed in 1282, and Wales became an English colony. The experience of the Welsh under English domination during the fourteenth century inspired the development of a more clearly defined national consciousness. Such was certainly displayed in the truly national rebellion of 1400, led by Owain Glyndwr. Wales was becoming recognized as one of the nations of Europe, although its cultural nature was changing, notably in abandonment of traditional Welsh law. After Glyndwr's rebellion, independence from England ceased to be a possibility, but Welsh influence within a joint Anglo-Welsh polity grew, not least with the accession to the English throne of the Welsh Henry Tudor in 1485.

From the twelfth century to the present day, all or part of Ireland has been controlled, more or less strongly, from Britain. The initial Norman intervention in Ireland – like the Roman invasion of Britain in AD 43 – was at the request of a local ruler seeking support. Dermot MacMurrough appealed to Henry II in 1166. A group of Norman warlords from Wales were soon out of control, conquering parts of Ireland on their own behalf. Henry II, alarmed at the prospect of an independent Norman kingdom in Ireland, arrived in person in 1171, receiving the submission of Irish rulers as well as Normans. For the Irish leaders, submission to a distant monarch promised security through royal control of the rampaging Norman lords, and did not appear as a 'sell-out' of Irish liberties. Patchy but quite intensive colonization during the thirteenth century made Ireland England's first overseas colony, and brought growing resistance by Irish leaders, leading to a three-way contest between the partly Gaelicized Anglo-Norman lords, indigenous rulers and the English crown. The last of these, by the fifteenth century, controlled only a shrinking area around Dublin. Most of Ireland was controlled by Gaelic or Gaelicized rulers who took little notice of royal power. As in Britain, identity and affiliation in Ireland remained complex. The originally Norse city of Dublin, for instance, a well-established part of Irish Sea commercial networks, looked as much towards Chester and Bristol as across Ireland.

While the threat of English royal power prompted resistance and redefinition of identities among her smaller insular neighbours, continental conflicts with even more powerful France did the same for the English. The Hundred Years War, from the mid-fourteenth to the mid-fifteenth century, started as a dynastic conflict within the French-speaking transnational aristocratic network established on either side of the Channel. But the destructiveness and growing bitterness of the conflict (caused not least by the dominance of despised English and Welsh archers over French chivalry) helped to forge a new self-aware Englishness spanning ethnic/class divisions: significantly, the nobility switched their speech from French to English. Reciprocally, the devastation caused by English soldiers in France helped precipitate the development of a sense of French national identity.

In summary, it may be argued that, in the islands, national self-consciousness as we understand it today – that is, an awareness of common identity and particular traits shared by most members of society no matter what their social standing – started to come into being during the later Middle Ages. It should also be noted that, while they fiercely contested their rights not to be subsumed into England, there seem to have been no signs of any particular fellow-feeling between the 'Celtic' nations. Robert the Bruce, for instance, took his war against England into Ireland, but intrigued with both the indigenous and English colonist communities. He played both the 'common Gaelic heritage' and the 'trans-national nobility' cards.

THE RENAISSANCE AND EARLY MODERN PERIOD
(*c*.1500–*c*.1800)

After 1500 the political history of the islands was increasingly determined in London, as England's growing military and commercial muscle raised her towards the status of a world power. The beginnings of an English trans-oceanic empire in the seventeenth century had great potential implications for the non-English nations: rapprochement with London promised, at least to certain groups, access to a share of the imperial cake. Major processes within and between the peoples of the isles raised new issues of identity, as Wales became a peripheral province of England (unified 1536–43), Scotland and England came to be jointly ruled by the Stuart (Stewart) house (from 1603), and in Ireland the autonomy of the last Gaelic rulers was crushed (1607), to be followed by heavy Anglo-Scottish colonization.

These new political interactions were strongly impacted by convulsions in one of the most important domains of identity and cultural affiliation: religion. By the end of the sixteenth century, the Reformation left Britain predominantly and permanently Protestant (albeit with fierce doctrinal divisions of its own), while Ireland, just as resolutely, remained largely Catholic. Religion was reopened as a dimension for ethnic or national distinction and conflict with a bitterness hardly seen since the Viking period.

Equally long-term in its effects, many of which would only be fully felt in the following centuries, was the European Renaissance. Ideas and attitudes learned from Greek and Roman sources underpinned the development of centralized states, while the narratives of authors such as Caesar formed the basis for a new Europe-wide interest in national origins and of more scientific attempts to investigate them. A new historical awareness, combined with changes in political philosophy, saw the beginnings of modern-style national self-consciousness. This is the context of Pezron and Lhuyd, scholars who were promoting the standing of the Bretons, the Welsh and their non-English neighbours among the nations of Europe.

Royal absolutism through the seventeenth and eighteenth centuries saw the long-term decline of aristocratic power, the increasing involvement in political thought and action of the lesser landed gentry, and the rise of the commercial and industrialist classes. Before the eighteenth century was out, the American and French revolutions marked the appearance of mass patriotism, with its notions of national identity, solidarity, citizenship and historical roots embracing all classes of society to an unprecedented degree. This was a major contrast with the states of the *ancien régime*, where obedience more than personal commitment and participation was expected of the masses. These revolutionary trends had a profound influence on the peoples of the islands.

The accession of James VI/I and the Scottish Stuarts to the English throne in 1603 did not lead to union with England, for mutual hostilities ran deep. They continued to be marked not least in the field of religion, after the Reformation as before it, and were a major factor in the wars which racked Britain during the 1640s. James VI/I did not succeed in his desire to be a *British* rather than an Anglo-Scottish king, but the idea of supra-national identities was in the air. Yet even the Treaty of Union of 1707, carried by the political and religious interests of sections of the politically active classes in Scotland, did not reconcile many Scots to a new British identity for another lifetime. It only really became established in England and Scotland after the loss of the American colonies in the 1770s, with the development of a second 'British Empire' based on India. Profitable participation in the imperial adventure gave Scotland growing reason to remain in the Union. Internally, Scottish identity remained complex and fraught. The difference between Highlander and Lowlander was deep, and antagonism often intense, especially after the expulsion of the last Stuart king, James II, for his Catholicism. The destruction of Highland military power in the 1740s was not unwelcome to many other Scots. The Scottish Enlightenment, represented by figures such as David Hume and Adam Smith, established Edinburgh especially as a major centre of the wider British and European cultural scene, but thereby threatened to undermine Scottish distinctiveness.

In Ireland, from the 1530s English royal authority was increasingly asserted over the old Anglo-Irish nobles and Gaelic rulers alike. The last rebellious earls fled in 1607. Ireland, and especially Ulster, was subjected to large-scale implantation of English and Scots and expropriation of Catholics. Perhaps 100,000 colonists arrived by 1640. The two parallel communities were distinguished by religion more than by ethnic origin: the state and colonists were now Protestant, while the Irish – Gaelic and old Anglo-Irish alike – remained overwhelmingly Catholic. The Protestant establishment in Britain was permanently fearful of 'Popish plots' in Ireland benefiting the powerful continental Catholic states, and so Catholicism, and native Irishness, were regarded with increased fear, suspicion and prejudice. In the context of simmering civil conflict in Britain, a rising by some Catholic landowners in 1641 triggered an explosion of fury by the Catholic population against the Protestant colonists which, bloody enough, caused a paranoiac reaction. After the victory of the Parliamentarians in Britain, in 1649 Cromwell unleashed his army in Ireland, bringing the full horrors of the Wars of Religion and a shattering of the remaining Catholic landholding. The overthrow in London of the Catholic James II in 1688 led to a civil war fought not in Britain, but in Ireland, and resulted in the Protestant triumphs (as they have been remembered) of the defence of Londonderry and the victory of William of Orange at the Battle of the Boyne in 1690.

In 1700, then, Ireland was largely under the domination of recently arrived English (and in Ulster, largely Scottish) landowners, a case of 'élite domination' groups which were ethnically, and especially religiously, distinct. The mass expropriation of Catholic lands, which roused an evolving national consciousness, and the beginnings of a much more clearly defined sense of Irish ethnic identity among the oppressed peasantry and fragments of the old Gaelic gentry alike, fuelled a sense of the burning injustice of dispossession and the memory of former national glories. But ethnically, the Catholic population of Ireland was not entirely Gaelic: it included significant elements of Anglo-Norman origin. Nor, during the eighteenth century, was there the relatively well-defined equation of Protestantism with a desire to be part of a greater Britain, and Catholicism seeking Irish independence. Indeed, for much of the century, major elements of the Protestant Ascendancy, especially Dissenters (politically disabled like the Catholics), wanted more autonomy for Ireland, albeit in their own sectarian interests, while Catholics and their Church looked to London for such protection and gradual erosion of the political disabilities they suffered, as they could achieve.

Religion, then, was more important than ethnic origins in drawing the lines of a three-way struggle in eighteenth-century Ireland. At the end of the eighteenth century new political ideologies further confused patterns of affiliation and identity in Ireland. Attempts to challenge British power, and even to establish a republic in Ireland, were largely guided by Protestant radicals like Wolfe Tone, who was inspired by the French and American revolutions (the latter itself led by Protestant gentlemen against Westminster), although the confused rising which followed in 1798 was more an expression of Catholic frustration driven by economic distress than a clear patriotic revolution. The result, not least because it was prompted by an attempted French invasion, was overreaction from London and enforced union with Britain in 1801. With such a mixture of religions, ethnic backgrounds, languages and political and economic interests, the nature of Irishness was far from simple.

THE NINETEENTH AND TWENTIETH CENTURIES

The Revolutionary and Napoleonic Wars formed the backdrop to the rise of Romanticism and romantic nationalism across Europe. The British Establishment was terrified of the revolutionary fervour seen in France, and ruthlessly repressed any such movements, notably in Ireland. But the cultural influence of Romanticism was felt throughout insular societies, and had highly varied effects on the peoples of the archipelago.

Within the islands themselves, massive economic changes brought on by the wars, the industrial revolution and contemporaneous agricultural developments resulted in major movements of people. Internal migration from countryside to cities and industrial zones massively affected all the peoples of the islands and altered the demographic map of the archipelago. Rural depopulation was felt most bitterly in the Scottish Highlands, where the destruction of clan society after the 1745 Rising culminated in the replacement of the people with more profitable sheep; and even more traumatic was the mass starvation and forced emigration of the swollen rural population of Ireland during the famine. Rural Wales and England were also profoundly affected. As well as moving to their own growing industrial centres, English migrants flocked into South Wales, while Catholic Irish went to Belfast and especially to cities such as Liverpool. Both Catholic and Protestant Irish migrated to Glasgow. Many Highlanders, too, ended up in these cities. There was even greater mass migration overseas, from all parts of the islands, but in percentage terms Scotland, Wales and especially Ireland were more deeply affected than England. The consequences of these upheavals for identities and politics were complex.

Unlike many other European peoples (and notably the Irish), the Scots did not develop a significant nationalist movement during the nineteenth century. This was primarily because of the huge economic benefits of partnership in British imperialism, which fuelled the industry of the Clyde in particular. However, Scots generally still retained a very strong sense of difference from England, which was notably expressed in the continued distinctiveness in religion and in its legal and education systems. Cultural expression of Scottishness was greatly influenced by the Romantic movement, which led to the paradoxical adoption of features of Highland culture as symbolic of Scottishness as a whole, even as this regional culture was being destroyed by the Clearances. The new confidence of the rising British middle classes in industrial progress, and the distancing of many from the countryside in new industrial cities, permitted the romanticization of the remote past, remote peoples and remote landscapes, because these were no longer perceived as threatening. After Culloden in 1746, the Highlanders ceased to be regarded as dangerous, but could be seen as a wild and romantic Other. This was expressed in the phenomenal enthusiasm for MacPherson's 'translations' of 'Ossian', a supposed ancient Highland bard, published during the 1760s, and then the Waverley novels of Sir Walter Scott in the early nineteenth century. It is ironic that Scott, a Borderer, should inextricably link Scottish identity with symbols of a shattered Highland society – tartan plaids and Highland pipes. It is also hard to exaggerate the impact that MacPherson, and later Scott, had on the cultural imagination not only of the peoples of the islands, but of Europe (particularly France and Germany). The consequent idealization and sentimentalization of Highland culture appealed to a broad range of social groups, not least among those Highlanders exiled to cities or overseas. However, in practical politics, Scotland was in general content to be 'North British'. Anti-imperialist, anti-English or Celtic nationalisms remained insignificant until after the Second World War. The loss of empire after that removed Scotland's main motivation for being content with the Union.

Wales presents a similar case to that of Scotland. Welsh identity was in more danger of being subsumed by Englishness during the eighteenth century, and in the nineteenth and early twentieth centuries much of Wales, especially the south, was, like Clydeside, benefiting from integration into the imperial industrial economy. Wales, too, was drastically affected by economic migration, from the countryside to the New World or to the mines and factories, where the Welsh were joined by a huge influx from England. This ethnic influx brought renewed tensions over the nature of Welsh identity and a growing threat to the Welsh language, increasingly a minority speech confined to certain regions.

The Welsh case also resembles Scotland in that the beginning of redefinition of Welsh identity was very much part of the Romantic movement, and that it was articulated in England as much as in Wales: indeed, it largely started among the expatriate London Welsh. The 1790s saw a Welsh literary and historical revival centred on the figure of Iolo Morganwg. For the first time in two hundred years this provided the Welsh with a coherent vision of their own history, as the basis for recreating a distinctive Welshness. It emphasized the 'rediscovery' of the ancient Druidic tradition and the running theme of Welsh struggle against English oppression. A new *gorsedd* (Order of Bards) was established as remembrancers of Welshness; *eisteddfodau* were reinvented; and a new Welsh national ideology was forged, drawing on the deep history which eighteenth-century philological and antiquarian scholarship was revealing. Morganwg invented 'traditions' and, like Macpherson in Scotland, wove fabrications with genuine discoveries which touched a public nerve.

Mid-nineteenth-century expressions of English chauvinism against Welsh speech and culture caused an angry reaction, leading to a Welsh cultural revival and reinvigoration of the National Eisteddfod. While many in the working-class communities engaged passionately in cultural activities (notably in the establishment of choirs), it was very much a middle-class movement, expressing a 'Welsh Welshness' which had little to say to many Welsh people (especially the English-speaking majority), to whom the Chapel and labour politics were of much greater significance. As in Scotland, until the Second World War Welsh national identity was still articulated within the framework of the United Kingdom: more separatist nationalism has only become significant since the 1960s and 1970s.

In Ireland agitation for the repeal of the Union was growing during the 1840s, a time of renewed revolutionary fervour across Europe. Drawing on the work of antiquaries which was helping to reveal the art and culture of pre-Norman, Christian Gaelic Ireland, the developing nationalist ideology was creating a history depicting the Irish people as struggling against foreign invaders while maintaining their cultural identity. While placing Catholic faith at its centre, it also drew on wider European trends of the period, which emphasized well-defined, long-established and immutable 'national characters' also seen in wider racial (and racist) discourse. This movement was dislocated by the horrors of the potato famine, mass starvation bringing death or enforced emigration to millions. Meanwhile, the socially stigmatized Irish language was pushed into decline by emigration and the developing market economy, although industrialization was largely confined to Belfast, a city of Presbyterians albeit with a growing Catholic proletariat.

Political emancipation of Catholics saw the entrenching of sectarian politics, with the Catholic Church more and more firmly associated with nascent nationalism, and evangelical Protestantism with the tradition that would later become Unionist. Alongside constitutional politics more militant groups indulged in Anglophobic rhetoric (including the accusation that the famine had been deliberately engineered) and sporadic revolutionary activity. By 1870, the Protestant Ascendancy was effectively broken outside Ulster, and the Catholic Nationalist movement was maturing. Yet the lines were not yet as sharp as in the twentieth century, for it was under a Protestant leader, Charles Parnell, that Nationalist electoral power seemed close to winning Home Rule from Westminster in 1886. It failed, but constitutional Nationalism continued.

The 1890s saw a significant cultural revival. The Gaelic League, founded in 1893, focused an attempt to de-Anglicize Ireland by reviving the Irish language and promoting entertainments deemed 'Irish', including traditional music, poetry recitations and history lectures. Initially nonsectarian, the League was taken over by Fenians (members of the revolutionary movement the Irish Republican Brotherhood), and the Irish-Ireland movement as a whole became closely tied to Sinn Féin. As David Fitzpatrick has commented, 'The political significance of the Irish-Ireland movement consisted . . . in the training and ideology with which it equipped a small knot of enthusiasts who by a strange accident came to dominate nationalism after 1916' (Fitzpatrick 1992, p. 186). The triumph of such a strongly Gaelic ideological base for free Ireland was thus not inevitable, but the result of historical contingency. Urban Protestantism in Ulster reacted militantly to further attempts at securing Home Rule, and in 1912 Ireland stood on the brink of civil war. The European cataclysm of 1914 put the issue on hold – or so most people thought.

The Easter Rising of 1916 was the work of a small group of militants who intended to create martyrs, to try to trigger greater Nationalist militancy. The rising was quickly and bloodily crushed with little initial public sympathy, but succeeded in its aims due to the overreaction of the British government to 'treason' in the midst of a war, by executing leading rebels and making indiscriminate arrests. Constitutional impasse from 1918 resulted in a War of Independence, culminating in partition of the Protestant-dominated North from the Catholic-dominated bulk of the island, which itself triggered civil war in the South. The ideology of the new state which emerged during the 1920s and 1930s drew directly on the Irish-Ireland movement. It sought to promote Gaelic as the primary official language, and filled the school history curriculum with Gaelic values and exemplars. The attempted language revival was a failure, but the 'Gaelicization' of Irish historical identity, emphasis on Celtic roots and the marginalization of most post-Norman elements were considerably more successful.

English identity has rarely been an active issue in recent times, while England remained the dominant partner in a 'British' United Kingdom, itself the centre of a world empire. The dismantling of that empire has resulted in radical changes in the situation of England, as of the other insular nations. Over the last two or three centuries England has been the major recipient of migrants from within the archipelago, and also the main destination for new ethnic groups from outside (although of course important new communities have been established in urban centres across the isles). From the Huguenots in the seventeenth century to the East European Jews of nineteenth-century London and the new 'ethnic minority' communities of Afro-Caribbean, Chinese and Indian sub-continent peoples of Hindu, Sikh and Muslim identity, and many other groups established in major cities since the 1950s, immigration has enormously enriched and diversified the human map of the islands. Combined with the reorientation of the insular economy towards continental Europe and growing centrifugal tendencies within the UK, immigration has radically altered the circumstances of Englishness. There have been important manifestations of right-wing chauvinism and hostility towards immigrants and the European Union in particular, ranging from Tory 'Little Englandism' to sporadic outbreaks of fascist politics. However, it is only with the realization of devolution for Wales and Scotland, and the genuine prospect of Scottish independence leading to the political break-up of Britain, that overt discussions of the current nature of Englishness have become more frequent.

Even today, then, in the Europe of nations, the ideas of boundedness and easily defined homogeneous identities are mirages. England, for example now has a highly diverse ethnic mix, making the nature of Englishness a moot point. In Scotland, a sense of *difference* from England and the English remains fundamental, as it was in 1300. But what actually *is* Scottishness, beyond non-Englishness (the kind of self-distinction from 'Them' at the basis of all such identities)? Scotland remains internally complex, as it has always been, seen in the twin religious traditions of Glasgow and the tensions between institutional Edinburgh and the regions, not least the Scandinavian-derived distinctiveness of the Northern Isles.

RETROSPECT AND PROSPECT

It is possible to discern a long-term trend in the ethnic and national history of the isles. Starting with later prehistoric populations hardly differentiated at all into well-defined, durable 'ethnic' identity groups, there was a patchy movement towards a churning kaleidoscope of very small units, more and more of which linked together to become unstable 'tribal' agglomerations during the later Iron Age. This was followed before, during and after the Roman episode by gradual coalescence into a collection of many small states, often quite loosely organized and short-lived, leading by later medieval times to the familiar national groups we still see today. Supra-national notions like shared Britishness and shared Celticness only became established relatively recently. Overall, then, we can see a pattern of larger and larger socio-political identity groups, created partly by the merging of existing entities (forming the historic kingdoms), sometimes by the accretion of an extra tier of identity linking smaller units which continued to exist. The uppermost scale of shared identity and action in the archipelago developed in the eighteenth century, expressing itself constitutionally as 'Britain' and the 'United Kingdom', and culturally and politically as 'the Celtic peoples'. Emergence of such pan- or supra-national identities was a widespread phenomenon in European societies of the time, culminating in the rise of new nation-states from hitherto fragmented peoples (Germany, Italy) and also in the conceptualization of wider contemporary associations of peoples by 'race' or 'nation', such as the 'Celtic' and 'Nordic' or 'Teutonic' worlds.

A long-term, generally directional trend, then, may be traced, towards larger scales of socio-political organization, albeit fitful, sometimes extremely rapid, in many areas marked by long periods of continuity and slow change, and locally not always in the same direction: the catastrophic collapse of Roman Britain is a good example of this. It has been a progression, but not necessarily 'progress': whether it marks improvement rather than just change is a matter of opinion (there are always losers as well as winners).

We tend to envision the named groupings which arose during the last

2,000 years as being like those of our own world, where secular national identities predominate; this is how we organize our wider societies and our politics, as nation-states with national broadcasting networks and newspapers. But before the nineteenth century, how 'real' were all these units in terms of mass engagement, of popular participation outside the groups with power? How far were they the artificial impositions of the ambitious, and how far expressions of the cultural consciousness of self-aware peoples?

Ethnicity and nationhood depend on *self*-identity, on being aware of larger groupings and their interactions, and feeling *involved* in one of them. I would argue that, until the rise of the four historic nations in the medieval period, and even long after, a clear sense of large-scale ethnic or national identity – of belonging to an imagined community like the Scots, Welsh, Irish or English – was usually weakly developed among the mass of the people, who rarely had to deal with such issues on hills or farms or in island fishing communities. Among the bulk of the populations of Britain and Ireland, it seems to me that at least until the sixteenth century any adherence to wider 'imagined communities' beyond their immediate district was more likely to be to a religion than to a major ethnicity or nation. Since the later Iron Age the societies of the isles have mostly been strongly hierarchical, dominated by élites operating at an increasingly 'international' level. Ethnic units and the boundaries between them remained primarily the concern of those with power – the aristocracy and gentry. The engagement of the bulk of the population in, and their identification with, the negotiations and conflicts of these groups were usually very limited. For example, down to the end of the eighteenth century, as elsewhere in Europe, even ordinary soldiers serving in royal armies were simply expected to obey their social superiors and to be loyal to the monarch, not to be participants, to feel ideologically committed to 'people', 'nation' or 'state'.

Even among social élites, commitment to a national or ethnic ideal was often much less important than religious identity or their personal standing in systems of status, rank and privilege which transcended ethnic boundaries. Often the action of nobles was more likely to be determined by religious and dynastic politics than a concern for ethnic divisions, which some nobility and royalty might give their lives for, while their peers often crossed them with ease. Examples include 'élite mobility' – magnates moving interchangeably from country to country at most periods from the Iron Age to the medieval era – and the religious conflicts which cut across ethnicity and nation during the Reformation (profoundly and permanently in the cases of Ireland and Scotland).

Mass engagement in ethnic identities may well have been seen at particular junctures in the past, when, at least for a period, a much deeper sense of solidarity may be inferred between nobles and commoners, specifically in the face of an alien threat. Examples include the Boudican revolt against the Romans, responses to the fury of the Vikings, and Irish reactions to Anglo-Scottish colonization from the seventeenth century. However, it is notable that in these cases it was religion which constituted the principal focus of difference.

It is only with the development of the nation-state over the last five centuries, and especially with the decline of the power of land-owning nobilities and the Church and the rise of the citizen, that large-scale ethnicities or national identities, adhered to jointly by people of all classes, have appeared in Northern Europe. A sense of *mass* patriotism, with all its symbols, including particular ethnic conceptions of the past, which in the twentieth century has been evoked by such words as 'Irish', 'Welsh', or 'British', finds its appearance no earlier than the time of the American and French revolutions. It was spawned by the particular historical trajectories of Europe, combining larger populations, more intensive long-distance contacts, more access to news about the world. Above all, people were exposed to new nationalist ideologies.

The contrast between the older, small-scale, hierarchical societies and the modern mass, national societies which gave rise to our present notions of identity may be seen by comparing two broadly contemporaneous cases: the Scottish Highlanders in the century following the 1745 Rising and the French during the Revolution and the Napoleonic era.

During the nineteenth century, the Highlands were largely deliberately depopulated by landlords to make room for more profitable stock raising. The people of the Highlands did not militantly organize on any significant scale to resist their piecemeal expulsion from their homelands. The reason for this is probably to be sought in the traditional organization of Highland society, in which members of the clans were deeply dependent on their social superiors, through personal ties of loyalty and subordination. The abandonment of their paternalistic obligations to their dependants by most clan chiefs was a result of their more or less willing integration into wider British economic and political structures after 1745. It left the bulk of the population without the ideological structures or the social networks necessary to organize, redefine themselves and resist, and without the time to develop these before they were expelled. Traditional Highland society reveals the kind of pattern which was probably typical of most insular societies from the Iron Age to the early modern period; one in which, outside their local community, the bulk of the population were largely excluded by the powerful from major questions of ethnic or national identity and large-scale communal interaction.

Contrast this with the fiery motivation and solidarity of French revolutionary citizen-soldiers, indoctrinated with an ideology of personal participation as citizens of the French nation, as *enfants de la patrie* – imagery which was itself partly drawn from heroic notions of France's Celtic, Gallic past (Ossian was enormously popular in France, too). The power of this ideology created highly motivated armies which smashed the professional royal forces of continental Europe.

These examples reveal the real contrast between modern and earlier notions of group identity, and the dangers of interpreting the distant past in terms of recent nationalist mentalities

If Celticness really is a phenomenon of the age of the nation-state and of supra-national groupings, what is its future? Especially if, as seems likely, we are in the midst of the break-up of the United Kingdom, which, with hindsight, we may decide has been under way for a lifetime, with Irish independence as the first step? Or are we just seeing the continuation of the fitful trend towards larger units in the isles and Europe as a whole, the negotiation of a new disposition which will accommodate a fully developed additional tier of identity, with 'European-ness' becoming a national identity, if not an ethnic one? In a federal Europe, will a sense of Celticness develop as a regional cultural manifestation, or will it fade with the proportional diminishing of English influence in a wider federation? In terms of the development of identities in these islands, we are living in interesting times.

6 Conclusion: Are the Modern Celts Bogus?

Men run with great avidity to give their evidence in favour of what flatters their passions and their national prejudices.

> (David Hume to Edward Gibbon, on the inauthenticity
> of the Celtic poems of Ossian, 18 March 1776)

As the previous chapters have shown, the idea of a race, nation or ethnic group called Celts in Ancient Britain and Ireland is indeed a modern invention. It is an eighteenth- and nineteenth-century 'reification' of a people that never existed, a factoid (a theoretical construct masquerading as fact) assembled from fragments of evidence drawn from a wide range of societies across space and time. This reification served the interests of a range of cultural expectations, aspirations and political agendas – and still does. Yet, as a model for understanding the past, it fails adequately to explain the available evidence, especially the rich archaeological testimony for the insular Iron Age.

'The Celts', then, must be rejected as an ethnic label for the populations of the islands during the Iron Age, the Roman period or indeed medieval times, not least in the direct sense that they did not use this name for themselves. The name is also to be rejected in the more general sense, in that it implies that culturally the Iron Age populations of Ireland and Britain were 'really' all the same kind of people (which is here challenged), and that they were all essentially the same as the continental Celts (who are themselves hard to define and probably also largely a reification). Further, the term 'Celtic' has accumulated so much baggage, so many confusing meanings and associations, that it is too compromised even to be useful as a more general label for the culture of these periods. The peoples in question organized themselves in a diversity of ways, made and used material culture in many different ways, and, it seems, spoke a variety of languages and dialects, which were not all mutually intelligible. The undoubted similarities and relations between them are best explained in terms of parallel development of many societies in intimate contact, rather than of radiation from a recent single common origin. It is inappropriate to give them a single, shared name, whether 'Celts' or any other; if they had clear group identities at all, these were manifold and changing. To the question, 'what, then, should we call the peoples of early Britain and Ireland?', the answer must be, exactly that: 'the peoples of Britain and Ireland'. To give them a single name is almost as pointless as asking what is the ethnicity (singular) of the population of Asia.

Yet, as we have seen, the idea of the existence of modern Celts in the British Isles has always been predicated on the assumption that they were the direct descendants of Ancient Celts in these lands. Since the Ancient Celts appear to have spurious historical roots, does it not follow that the modern Celts, too, must be bogus? Paradoxically, the answer is 'No'. Discrediting the insular Ancient Celts does not make the modern Celts fraudulent. For the more sophisticated understandings of the nature of ethnic identities now available to us, which reveal the Ancient Celts to be a modern construct, equally suggest that the modern Celts constitute a perfectly real and legitimate 'ethnic group'. The resolution of this paradox lies in chronology: the modern Celts are not the present representatives of a people who have existed continuously for millennia, but constitute a true case of 'ethnogenesis' – the birth of an ethnic identity – in *early modern* Europe.

As we have seen, the study of ethnic identities reveals a number of recurrent themes:

- *They arise from a sense of shared difference, and usually perceived threat, from another group with which they are in contact.* In the case of the Welsh, Scots, Irish and others, this common cultural Other was England which, with the drive towards a basically English, uniform 'Britishness' following the Union of 1707, and the incorporation of Ireland in 1801, threatened to swamp other cultural traditions.
- *They express their identity by attaching symbolic value to aspects of their culture deemed characteristic.* In defining themselves, ethnic groups choose particular aspects of their culture which they share in common, but which the Other lacks, and invest them with symbolic significance. The choice of these symbols depends on the cultural make-up of the group, and the particular historical circumstances prevailing at the time. Language is often of fundamental importance, and we have seen that it was possession of a distinctive group of

related languages that formed the touchstone for the new Celtic identity. However, the Celts are apparently unique in defining themselves in terms of a group of *mutually unintelligible* languages. This idea only became conceivable as a result of the development of philology and the work of Pezron and Lhuyd. Before this, the notion of such a language family was unthought of and literally unthinkable. Here is a remarkable example of the historical contingency of ethnic self-definition.

- *Such groups also choose an 'ethnonym'*, in the present case one derived from the label invented for their newly discovered shared characteristic, their related languages, which semi-arbitrarily were labelled 'Celtic'. This determined that they were now to be called Celts, and retrospectively must always have been Celts (the fact that the term was not used before 1700 is usually glossed over).
- *Ethnic groups create an agreed common history through the selective use and reframing of traditions of pre-existing groups, or the simple invention, from scratch, of 'ancient' roots.* Much of this book has been about how both the modern Celts, and their English cultural Others, abetted by European scholars with parallel continental interests, shared in creating just such a historical pedigree for the insular Celts. Their linguistic affiliations, and also early interpretations of archaeological remains, apparently gave the insular Celts a remarkably long continuous history, back into pre-Roman continental Europe. That this tradition of historiography is now under attack does not invalidate *modern* Celtic identity, because to some degree *all* modern ethnic and national identities create essentially propagandist histories like this - not least the English, and the British state.

But perhaps the clearest evidence for the reality of the *modern* insular Celts is the simple fact that millions of people feel themselves to be in some sense Celtic.

The concept of British identity, although apparently so different from that of the Celts, has some interesting similarities with it. It, too, was a new creation from pre-existing components – the political and religious structures of the existing kingdoms. It, too, was created in response to perceived outside threats. It, too, chose a name redolent with antiquity (its citizens being 'Britons', also harking back to pre-Roman times). It, too, created (and creates) its own history, traditions and rituals to give an impression of antiquity which is often spurious. The exact present meaning, and importance, of 'Britishness' to many nominally British people is also as highly problematic as the 'Celticness' of the nominally Celtic peoples. To many, Britishness seems to mean less than older national or regional identities, as devolution and the resurgence of Scottish and Welsh nationalism demonstrate. Indeed, at the end of the twentieth century, it can be argued that the question mark hanging over the present validity and future prospects of Britishness, and the existence of the largely political entity called 'Britain', is bigger than that hanging over the modern Celts.

CELTS, SCHOLARS, AND MOTIVES

If the insular Ancient Celts did not exist, were the people who created them self-deluding fools, inasmuch as they looked into the past and saw only what they expected to see – a world conforming to their own un-acknowledged expectations and prejudices, and to their aspirations for history's legitimation of a newly created ('rediscovered') identity? Or were they knaves, deliberately misrepresenting the past and knowingly producing slanted histories to use as propaganda to advance their own political agendas? It seems to me that there is no reason to conclude that they were either of these cardboard caricatures. As Stephen Jay Gould has observed in words equally relevant to history and archaeology,

Science is no inexorable march to truth, mediated by the collection of objective information and the destruction of ancient superstition. Scientists, as ordinary human beings, unconsciously reflect in their theories the social and political constraints of their times.

(Gould 1980, p. 15)

Beyond unconscious bias or wish-fulfilment, discourse about the Celts has often involved a knowing cultural/political agenda, particularly since personal identity is at stake. But even if some felt inclined to study subjects, and knowingly to promote ideas, which favoured their wider cultural aspirations – as, I believe, Lhuyd himself sought to promote the interests of the Welsh and other non-English peoples of the isles – this does not inevitably invalidate or devalue their work. We need to understand the historical context within which these scholars were writing: we can then decide for ourselves what insights of lasting value they have made and where they may have misled us.

Looking at their work in the context of their own times, for me at least, leads to an understanding of why they thought the way they did, and promotes a growing admiration for their determination, skills and achievements. We can learn from them, even as we disagree with them. For of course early advocates of a Celtic past achieved many genuine and vital insights which are still accepted beyond question (such as the close relationships between the non-English insular tongues), even if many of their further inferences (that these equated with clearly defined ethnic Celtic invaders) were based on ideas now regarded as erroneous (especially theoretical assumptions about the nature of peoples and cultural change).

In discovering that our forerunners were constrained in their thinking by the assumptions, and blinkered by the prejudices, of their own times, we should not crow at our own presumed enlightened superiority; for surely the most important lesson is that scholars are always subject to these limitations and biases. We, too, labour under such constraints.

We can claim, with some confidence, that we genuinely know the insular Iron Age much more intimately now than we did fifty years ago. We can argue that the new ideas do constitute a better representation of the Iron Age past and therefore the origins of the Celtic present, since they explain more closely and coherently a much larger, broader, richer and better-explored body of evidence. Further, they explain it in terms of more sophisticated frameworks of understanding, themselves drawn from observations of many actual human groups – observations which contradicted expectations and so are unlikely to be artefacts of the observers' assumptions. All this gives us a far better feel for the shape and complexities of the subject. In this sense, progress has undoubtedly been made. Yet current ideas, like all past interpretations, are inevitably partial in both senses – incomplete, and not impartial.

The traditional, constructed story of the Celts is an example of 'Whig history'. It projects recent systems of thought and values into the past, which is implicitly represented as inevitably giving rise to the present existence of Celticness, from already recognizable Celtic roots in Antiquity; and it presents as objective and neutral what is actually a highly political view of history, rooted in nationalist politics. As we have seen, the different conception of the past which is presented here is equally situated in a particular cultural and political context, that of the late twentieth-century post-colonial, multi-cultural world. As such, it, too, is open to the charge that it is simply looking into the past and seeing a mirror image of itself. It does differ in a number of respects, as noted above; but, perhaps most importantly, it is considerably more aware of, and open about, its own situation. In this it is unlike the 'Celticist' model, which is usually presented as established fact, whereas it is actually a theoretical construct. The (for want of a more elegant term) 'post-Celticist' view makes the basis of its approach, and its conclusions, accessible to the kind of critical scrutiny and testing which is fundamental to the development of good scholarship. As Herbert Butterfield wrote in *The Whig Interpretation of History* (1931):

It is not a sin in a historian to introduce a personal bias that can be recognized and discounted. The sin in historical composition is the organization of the story in such a way that bias cannot be recognized.

Although an intensely human enterprise with its own high emotions, scholarship at its best is self-critical and self-correcting. It is always changing, and we have to accept that any statement is provisional and transient. Whether the views presented here of ethnicity in general, and of the insular Celts in particular, will prove durable, or will be wholly discredited as the wish-fulfilment of the post-colonial academic generation, remains to be seen.

Certainly, inadequacies are apparent to many 'post-Celticists', who are by no means uniform in their outlook. For example, some feel that the reaction against the assumption of essential uniformity of Iron Age societies has gone too far the other way. We might anticipate that, once we have worked through the full implications of the current emphases on variation and diversity, in the future the very real connections and commonalities, not just across the isles but also across Europe, will probably receive more attention again. But in the meantime, it is probably necessary to maintain 'clear blue water' between the old normative Celticism and its alternatives, to establish clearly the antithesis, to point up the inadequacies of established views, and to avoid being drawn back into the Celtic quagmire of confused meanings.

Realizing the influence of wider cultural and political trends on current ideas, and admitting it 'up-front', is, then, a genuine advance. Ruth and Vincent Megaw have recently suggested that current critiques of the Celts are an attack by nationalist, Little Englander archaeologists terrified of the threat to English hegemony in Britain posed by devolution and increasing European integration. I hope it is clear from the foregoing how profoundly wrong such interpretations are. Current archaeological discourse reflects its grounding in the world of post-colonial, multi-cultural thought. Emphasis on the complexity, diversity and probable multiplicity of identities in the Iron Age is also in harmony with the rest of our known history – that the populations of the islands have *always* been 'multi-cultural' and apparently 'multi-ethnic', comprising numbers of interacting identity groups.

Further, the idea of insular Ancient Celts is not being singled out for special attack. Celticity has rooted itself in a particular reading of the Iron Age, and so any work on the period automatically feeds back into discourse on Celts. Scrutiny of Celticity is actually just one facet of a range of similar critiques of other familiar 'peoples' in our past, and/or our present, currently under way in Britain and elsewhere. A similar critique of 'Britishness' by historians has already been alluded to. Conceptions of Ancient Rome, too, are currently subject to radical deconstruction, both in the direct context of the Roman presence in the isles, and indirectly, regarding the uses the British have made of Rome in 'borrowing' it as a model for their own imperial aspirations. Another piece in the jigsaw, absolutely crucial to understanding the development of the other identities of the isles – and especially Celticness since it constituted the cultural 'Other' – is the case of the Anglo-Saxons/English. Historians have led the way, and medieval archaeologists are now actively engaged in deconstructing the invention of the Anglo-Saxons and of Englishness over the last thousand years, not least as part of wider modern notions of 'Nordic', 'Germanic' or 'Teutonic' racial identities. These ideas were once very popular, but, since the world wars and the excesses of Nazism ended English enchantment with modern German and imagined ancient Germanic culture, they have been quietly all but forgotten in England. Critique of the Celts by British academics, then, is to be seen as part of a far wider trend of post-colonial overhaul of *all* our received historical categories and ideas.

Speaking strictly for myself, I do have particular concerns about the use of the past in the present. Tracing the roots of the insular Celtic idea to the colonialism of England/Britain and ethnic/nationalist resistance of those who rejected assimilation and demanded the right to maintain their own identities, helps us to understand the past but also warns us about potential futures. Our identities in these islands, our origin myths and our national histories, were forged from conflict over the last thousand years and more. It is important to maintain these identities, but equally vital to recognize them for what they are: evolving cultural constructs, not primordial immutable truths about ourselves, our origins and our historic antagonists. It is manifestly obvious that relations between the peoples of the isles have often been violent and destructive, and indeed that conflict, and *fear* of, or contempt for, those who are different, have been fundamental to the very creation and development of identities. We face the dilemma that the justice of acknowledging and celebrating multiple identities may inadvertently emphasize fault-lines between groups which can become the foci of renewed conflict. There are, then, dangers in strengthening the divisions between the ancient nations again. The prospect of all the nations of the Atlantic archipelago being free and independent sovereign states under a nascent 'United States of Europe' has considerable attractions – so long as it can be made to work. But is there room for the 'new' ethnic minorities in this picture of revived national self-consciousness? And what happens to the peoples of the isles if European integration fails, as well it may?

I believe that we need to be very wary of *all* resurgent nationalisms in the islands, perhaps (given the history of the past thousand years) among the English more than among the other insular peoples. Nationalisms, if they become chauvinistic, commonly justify themselves through claims about history, often made at the expense of neighbours and internal minorities. This is why it is politically important to look critically at the ideas underpinning the national histories of the islands. It is vital that *all* claims to historical legitimacy, from whatever quarter, be open to critical scrutiny and not accepted simply because they are asserted now, or have been established a long time.

A CONTINUING DEBATE

The Ancient Celts of the isles, especially in the simplistic way they have been traditionally conceived, are definitively discredited, in British archaeology at least. It remains to be seen how far archaeologists will be able to dislodge them from conceptions of popular history. Scholars have lost much of the cultural authority which meant that men like Lhuyd would be listened to. Society in Britain, Ireland and the rest of the Western world now lacks the cultural homogeneity and hierarchy of authority which permitted his ideas to become universally accepted so quickly. Most would today much prefer the greater freedom of expression and resultant diversity to the conformism of the past, and feel that sceptical public treatment of scholarly pronouncements is a healthy thing (academics and scientists too easily enjoy the role of secular priesthood given them in the nineteenth century by T. H. Huxley in particular). But we must then swallow the irony that, in a world of cultural fragmentation, it is far more difficult for us today to challenge and hope to dislodge old, discredited ideas which our predecessors helped establish so successfully in the popular imagination. Yet we must try, and to stand a chance of displacing outmoded conceptions, any new alternative must be easily held in mind. In place of the motifs of Iron Age Celtic invaders, followed by 'Dark Age' Germanic ones, we must suggest other clear conceptions. The very complexity of the issues makes this hard to achieve. However, I would suggest the following: the isles have always been home to many peoples, who have fought one another, but also drawn on one another; these peoples have created themselves and also *created each other*, through their contacts and conflicts, and the islands have always been open to newcomers, who have added to life and modified the course of our shared histories.

The traditional 'story of the island Celts' is exactly that: a story, one of many possible histories which may be written as we struggle to make sense of the fragmentary testimony from the lost past. It is a version which simply does not accord with either the specific evidence for the case, or with general observation of the way the world works. Prior assumption that we know what the past was like buries without consideration the possibility that it may have been different. Imposing Celtic uniformity on the past denies earlier peoples any prospect of revealing to us their true sense of their identity, through the traces they have left of their lives. Prejudged as Celts, they are forced into a mould. This is ironic, since in origin modern Celticness was about asserting identity and difference in the present. Projecting Celtic identity back onto past societies which would neither have recognized nor understood it, obscures the real, complex history of the isles. At the very least, the critique presented here, and the different interpretations suggested, mean that we now have a choice of competing 'Celticist' and 'post-Celticist' interpretations to test against the evidence, which has to be better than the comfortable but stale consensus that has prevailed for so long.

GLOSSARY

A guide to some of the technical terms and usages employed in this book

Celt* 'I. *Hist.* Applied to the ancient peoples of Western Europe, called by the Greeks *Keltoí, Kéltai,* and by the Romans *Celtae.* 2. A general name applied in modern times to peoples speaking languages akin to those of the ancient Gauls, including the Bretons of France, the Cornish, Welsh, Irish, Manx and Gaelic of the British Isles.'

Celtic* 'I. *Hist & Archaeol.* Of or belonging to the ancient Celtae and their presumed congeners. 2. Epithet of the languages and peoples akin to the ancient Celtic; particularly, of the great branch of the Aryan family of languages which includes Breton, Welsh, Irish, Manx, Scotch Gaelic, the extant Cornish, and the ancient tongues which they represent . . .'

ethnic group** Any group of people who set themselves apart from others, on the basis of their perceptions of cultural difference and/or common descent.

ethnic identity** That aspect of a person's self-conceptualization which results from identification with a broader group in opposition to others, on the basis of *perceived* cultural difference and/or *perceived* common descent.

ethnicity** All those social and psychological phenomena associated with a culturally constructed group identity as defined above; the ways in which social and cultural processes are involved in the identification of, and interaction between, ethnic groups.

factoid An unproven idea or assumption that is repeated so often that it becomes accepted as factual truth.

Iron Age The name given by archaeologists to the last phase of prehistory, before the literate, historical era begins with the arrival of the Romans (during the first century AD in southern Britain). Iron appeared as the major tool- and weapon-making metal, displacing copper alloys, around the 700s BC in Britain, perhaps a little later in Ireland.

linguistics* The scientific study of languages and their structure [especially in the contemporary world, cf. PHILOLOGY].

material culture All the physical aspects of human life and society, from portable artefacts such as items of dress to equipment of production and structures such as houses, cities, etc.

normative Of, or establishing, a norm, which is a standard pattern or type.

paradigm An example or pattern, especially one underlying a theory or methodology: a mental model of how something works.

philology* The science of language, especially in its historical and comparative aspects [cf. LINGUISTICS].

reify, reification to convert an abstraction into a thing.

---

* Definitions taken from the *Oxford English Dictionary*, 2nd edn, 1989.
** Definitions taken, with modifications, from those given by Jones 1997, p. xiii.

FURTHER READING

CHAPTER 1 THE DEBATE ON CELTIC IDENTITY

General books on the ancient Celtic world: Cunliffe 1997; Green 1995; James 1993a; Kruta *et al.* 1991; Powell 1958.

The debate about archaeologists' motivations: Megaw and Megaw 1996; James 1998; Megaw and Megaw 1998.

Modern France and the Celtic Gauls, and the Celticness of Brittany: Dietler 1994.

The Venice exhibition on the Celts: Kruta *et al.* 1991.

The 'Celtic diaspora', e.g. the small Welsh community in Patagonia: Williams 1991; the Scots in Canada: Craig 1990.

A critique of the idea of 'Celtic spirit': Merriman 1987.

Druids: Piggott 1985a; Green 1997.

Early Christian illuminated manuscripts: Henderson 1987.

'Celtic art': Kruta *et al.* 1991; Megaw and Megaw 1989; Stead 1997.

Early literature, epic and myth in the Celtic languages: Green 1993; Jackson 1971.

Celtic languages: Ball 1993; Macauley 1992.

CHAPTER 2 STANDARD HISTORIES: ASSUMPTIONS, LIMITATIONS AND OBJECTIONS

Conventional histories of the Celts: e.g. James 1993a; Powell 1958.

Challenges to the conventional views of Celticness and insular Celtic history: Chapman 1992; Hill 1989; Renfrew 1996.

The invasionist 'ABC' scheme for the British Iron Age: Hawkes 1931, 1959.

Current views of the Iron Age. Ireland: O'Kelly 1989; Raftery 1994. Britain: Cunliffe 1991, 1995; Gwilt and Haselgrove 1997; Hill 1995b; James and Rigby 1997. Britain and Ireland: Hill 1995a. The wider European context: Collis 1984; Cunliffe 1988, 1997; Fitzpatrick 1996.

East Yorkshire burials: Stead 1991.

CHAPTER 3 HOW THE CELTS WERE CREATED, AND WHY

Archaeological theory: Johnson forthcoming.

Renaissance and early modern ideas on early Britain: Ferguson 1993; Piggott 1989.

Lhuyd: Emery 1971; Gunther 1945; Lhuyd 1707.
Celtic languages: Ball 1993; Macauley 1992.
Johnson and Boswell and Celts in Skye: Boswell 1786, p. 293.
Creation of British identity: Bradshaw and Morrill 1996; Colley 1992.
Romanticism and the development of interest in the Celts: Chapman 1992,
    chapter 9.
Classification of human groups, race, culture, and ethnicity: Jones 1997,
    chapter 3. Díaz-Andreu et al., in preparation.
Identifying and defining peoples in archaeology: Jones 1997.
Attack on invasionist interpretation of the insular Iron Age: Hodson 1964.

CHAPTER 4 CURRENT IDEAS ON ETHNICITY, AND THE INSULAR
ANCIENT CELTS
Ethnicity in the present and in the past: Jones 1997; Díaz-Andreu et al, in
    preparation.
Society and social practice: Bourdieu 1977; Giddens 1984.
Imagined communities: Anderson 1991.
The LoWiili: Goody 1967.
Pathans: Barth 1969.
Baringo district: Hodder 1982.
Roman military identity: James forthcoming.
Celtic languages: Macauley 1992; Ball 1993.
Celtic languages and ethnic history: Renfrew 1987, especially chapter 9;
Renfrew 1996.
On the past use and misuse of biological data: Gould 1981; Jones 1996.

CHAPTER 5 TOWARDS A NEW ETHNIC HISTORY OF THE ISLES
Current views of the Iron Age. Ireland: O'Kelly 1989; Raftery 1994. Scotland:
    Armit 1997. Britain: Cunliffe 1991, 1995; Gwilt and Haselgrove 1997; Hill
    1995b; James and Rigby 1997. Britain and Ireland: Hill 1995a. The wider
    European context: Collis 1984; Cunliffe 1988, 1997; Fitzpatrick 1996.
Regional diversity in the Iron Age: Cunliffe 1991.
Iron Age life: Cunliffe 1993.
Celtic art: Megaw and Megaw 1989; Stead 1997.
The parallel of pre-Roman Italian societies: Cornell 1995.
Rome and Britain: Millett 1990, 1995.
Free Caledonia: Armit 1997.
Ireland during Roman times: Raftery 1994.
Early medieval Ireland, Scotland, the Western Britons, and early Wales:
    Chadwick 1997.

The *Gododdin*: Jackson 1969.
Picts, Gaels, and the origins of Scotland: Foster 1996.
Medieval Scotland, and Scottish identity: Grant 1984; Webster 1997.
Scotland, from medieval to modern times: Lynch 1992.
Wales, from medieval to modern times: Williams 1985.
Ireland, from medieval to modern times: Foster 1992.
Ireland, the Gaelic/Celtic revival: Sheehy 1980; Hutchinson 1987.

CHAPTER 6 CONCLUSION: ARE THE MODERN CELTS BOGUS?
Nationalisms, archaeology of the idea of Celticity: Díaz-Andreu and Champion
    1996 (especially Champion 1996); Woodman 1995.
The political context of Irish archaeology: Woodman 1995; Cooney 1995.
The invention of national traditions, e.g. among the British, Welsh and Scots:
    Hobsbawm and Ranger 1983.
Creation of Britishness: Bradshaw and Morrill 1996; Colley 1992.
Critiques of the basis of Anglo-Saxon/English identity: MacDougall 1982; Lucy
    forthcoming a and b; Pohl 1997.
Deconstructing Roman imperialism: Webster and Cooper 1997.

BIBLIOGRAPHY

Anderson, B. 1991, *Imagined Communities: Reflections on the Origins and Spread of Nationalism*, rev. edn, Verso, London and New York.

Anthony, D. 1997, 'Prehistoric migrations as social process', in J. Chapman and H. Hamerow (eds), *Migrations and Invasions in Archaeological Explanation*, BAR International Series 664, pp. 21-32.

Armit, I. 1997, *Celtic Scotland*, Batsford/Historic Scotland, London.

Ball, M.J. (ed.) 1993, *The Celtic Languages*, Routledge, London and New York.

Barth, F. 1969, 'Pathan identity and its maintenance', in F. Barth (ed.), *Ethnic Groups and Boundaries*, Little Brown, Boston, pp. 9-38.

Boswell, J. 1786, *The Journal of a Tour to the Hebrides* (Penguin edn, Harmondsworth 1984).

Bourdieu, P. 1977, *Outline of a Theory of Practice.* Cambridge, Cambridge University Press.

Bradshaw, B., and Morrill, J. (eds) 1996, *The British Problem, c. 1534-1707: State Formation in the Atlantic Archipelago*, Macmillan, London and Basingstoke.

Butterfield, H. 1931, *The Whig Interpretation of History*, Bell, London.

Chadwick, N. 1997, *The Celts*, Penguin, Harmondsworth and New York.

Champion, T. 1996, 'Three nations or one? Britain and the national use of the past', in Díaz-Andreu and Champion 1996, pp. 119-45.

Chapman, M. 1992, *The Celts: The Construction of a Myth*, St Martin's Press, New York; Macmillan, London and Basingstoke.

Colley, L. 1992, *Britons: Forging the Nation 1707-1837*, Yale University Press, New Haven and London.

Collis, J. 1984, *The European Iron Age*, Batsford, London.

Collis, J. 1997, 'Celtic Myths', *Antiquity* LXXI, pp. 195-201.

Cooney, G. 1995, 'Theory and practice in Irish archaeology', in P. J. Ucko (ed.), *Theory in Archaeology: A World Perspective*, Routledge, London, pp. 263-77.

Cornell, T. 1995, *The Beginnings of Rome*, Routledge, London and New York.

Craig, D. 1990, *On the Crofters' Trail: In Search of the Clearance Highlanders*, Jonathan Cape, London.

Cunliffe, B.W. 1988, *Greeks, Romans and Barbarians*, Batsford, London.

Cunliffe, B.W. 1991, *Iron Age Communities in Britain*, 3rd edn, Routledge, London and New York.

Cunliffe, B.W. 1993, *Danebury: Anatomy of an Iron Age Hillfort*, rev. edn, Batsford/English Heritage, London.

Cunliffe, B.W. 1995, *English Heritage Book of the Iron Age*, Batsford/English Heritage, London.

Cunliffe, B.W. 1997, *The Ancient Celts*, Oxford University Press, Oxford and New York.

Díaz-Andreu, M., and Champion, T. (eds) 1996, *Nationalism and Archaeology in Europe*, UCL Press, London.

Díaz-Andreu, M., Graves, C.P., and Lucy, S.J., in preparation, *The Archaeology of Identity*, Routledge, London.

Dietler, M. 1994, '"Our ancestors the Gauls": archaeology, ethnic nationalism, and the manipulation of Celtic identity in modern Europe', *American Anthropologist* 96 (3), pp. 584-605.

Emery, F. 1971, *Edward Lhuyd 1660-1709*, Gwasg Prifysgol Cymru, Cardiff.

Ferguson, A.B. 1993, *Utter Antiquity: Perceptions of Prehistory in Renaissance England*, Duke University Press, Durham and London.

Fitzpatrick, A. 1996, '"Celtic" Iron Age Europe; the theoretical basis', in Graves-Brown *et al.* 1996, pp. 238-55.

Fitzpatrick, D. 1992, 'Ireland after 1870', in Foster 1992, pp. 174-239.

Foster, R.F. 1992, *The Oxford History of Ireland*, Oxford University Press, Oxford.

Foster, S.M. 1996, *Picts, Gaels and Scots*, Batsford/Historic Scotland, London.

Galliou, P., and Jones, M. 1991, *The Bretons*, Blackwell, Oxford and Cambridge, Mass.

Giddens, A. 1984, *The Constitution of Society*, Polity Press, Cambridge.

Goody, J. 1967, *The Social Organization of the LoWiili*, Oxford University Press, Oxford.

Gould, S.J. 1980, *Ever Since Darwin*, Penguin, Harmondsworth.

Gould, S.J. 1981, *The Mismeasure of Man*, Norton, New York and London.

Gould, S.J. 1991, *Bully for Brontosaurus*, Penguin, Harmondsworth.

Grant, A. 1984, *Independence and Nationhood: Scotland 1306-1469*, Edinburgh University Press, Edinburgh.

Graves-Brown, J., Jones, S., and Gamble, C. (eds) 1996, *Cultural Identity and Archaeology: The Construction of European Identities*, Routledge, London and New York.

Green, M.J. 1993, *Celtic Myths*, British Museum Press, London.

Green, M.J. (ed.), 1995, *The Celtic World*, Routledge, London.

Green, M.J. 1997, *Exploring the World of the Druids*, Thames & Hudson, London and New York.

Gunther, R.T. 1945, *Early Science in Oxford, Vol. XIV, Life and Letters of Edward Lhwyd*, Oxford University Press, Oxford.

Gwilt, A., and Haselgrove, C.C. (eds) 1997, *Reconstructing Iron Age Societies*, Oxbow, Oxford.

Hawkes, C. 1931 'Hill-forts', *Antiquity* v, pp. 60-97.

Hawkes, C. 1959, 'The ABC of the British Iron Age', *Antiquity* XXXIII, pp. 170-82.

Henderson, G. 1987, *From Durrow to Kells: The Insular Gospel Books, 650-800*, Thames & Hudson, London and New York.

Hill, J.D. 1989, 'Re-thinking the Iron Age', *Scottish Archaeological Review* 6, pp. 16-24.

Hill, J.D. 1995a, 'The Pre-Roman Iron Age in Britain and Ireland (ca. 800 B.C. to A.D. 100): an overview', *Journal of World Prehistory*, vol. 9, no. 1, pp. 47-98.

Hill, J.D. 1995b, *Ritual and Rubbish in the Iron Age of Wessex*, BAR British Series 242, Tempus Reparatum, Oxford.

Hobsbawm, E., and Ranger, T. (eds) 1983, *The Invention of Tradition*, Cambridge University Press, Cambridge.

Hodder, I. 1982, *Symbols in Action*, Cambridge University Press, Cambridge.

Hodson, F. R. 1964, 'Cultural groupings within the British pre-Roman Iron Age', *Proceedings of the Prehistoric Society* 30, pp. 99-110.

Hutchinson, J. 1987, *The Dynamics of Cultural Nationalism: The Gaelic Revival and the Creation of the Irish Nation State*, Allen & Unwin, London.

Jackson, K.H. 1969, *The Gododdin: The Oldest Scottish Poem*, Edinburgh University Press, Edinburgh.

Jackson, K.H. 1971, *A Celtic Miscellany*, Penguin, Harmondsworth.

James, S.T. 1993a, *Exploring the World of the Celts*, Thames & Hudson, London (= *The World of the Celts*, Thames & Hudson, New York).

James, S.T. 1993b, 'How was it for you? Personal psychology and the perception of the past', *Archaeological Review from Cambridge*, vol. 12, no. 2, pp. 87-100.

James, S.T. 1997, 'The Celts: discovery or invention?', *British Museum Magazine*, Summer 1997, pp. 18-22.

James, S.T. 1998, 'Celts, politics and motivation in archaeology', *Antiquity* LXXII, pp. 200-209.

James, S.T., forthcoming, 'The community of the soldiers: a major identity and centre of power in the Roman empire', in C. Forcey and B. Witcher (eds), *Proceedings of the Eighth Annual Theoretical Archaeology Conference, Leicester 1998*.

James, S.T., and Rigby, V. 1997, *Britain and the Celtic Iron Age*, British Museum Press, London.

Johnson, M., forthcoming, *Archaeological Theory: An Introduction*.

Jones, S. 1996, *In the Blood: God, Genes and Destiny*, Harper Collins, London.

Jones, S. 1997, *The Archaeology of Ethnicity: Constructing Identities in the Past and Present*, Routledge, London and New York.

Kruta, V., Frey, O., Raftery, B., and Szabo, M. (eds) 1991, *The Celts*, Thames & Hudson, London and New York.

Lhuyd, E. 1707, *Archaeologia Britannica, giving some account Additional to what has been hitherto Publish'd, of the Languages, Histories and Customs of the Original Inhabitants of Great Britain: From Collections and Observations in Travels through Wales, Cornwall [sic], Bas-Bretagne, Ireland and Scotland. Vol. I. Glossography*, Oxford.

Lucy, S., forthcoming a, 'Early medieval burials in East Yorkshire: re-considering the evidence', in H. Geake (ed.), *Anglo-Saxon Yorkshire* (conference proceedings).

Lucy, S., forthcoming b, 'Towards a contextual understanding of early Anglo-Saxon cemeteries', in M. Rundkvist (ed.), *Grave Matters: Provincial and Roman Burials in the First Millennium AD*.

Lynch, M. 1992, *Scotland: A New History*, rev. edn, Pimlico, London.

Macauley, D. (ed.) 1992, *The Celtic Languages*, Cambridge University Press, Cambridge.

MacDougall, H.A. 1982, *Racial Myth in English History: Trojans, Teutons and Anglo-Saxons*, Harvest House, Montreal; University Press of New England, Hanover and London.

Mattingly, D.J. 1997, 'Dialogues in Roman imperialism', *Journal of Roman Archaeology Supplementary Series*, no. 23.

Megaw, J.V.S., and Megaw, M.R. 1996, 'Ancient Celts and modern ethnicity', *Antiquity* LXX, pp. 175-81.

Megaw, J.V.S., and Megaw, M.R. 1998, 'The mechanism of (Celtic) dreams?: a partial response to our critics', *Antiquity* LXXII, pp. 432-5.

Megaw, M.R., and Megaw, J.V.S. 1989, *Celtic Art from its Beginnings to the Book of Kells*, Thames & Hudson, London and New York.

Merriman, N. 1987, 'Value and motivation in prehistory: the evidence for "Celtic spirit"', in Hodder, I. (ed.), *The Archaeology of Contextual Meanings*, Cambridge University Press, Cambridge, pp. 111-16.

Millett, M. 1990, *The Romanization of Britain*, Cambridge University Press, Cambridge.

Millett, M. 1995, *Roman Britain*, Batsford/English Heritage, London.

O'Kelly, M. 1989, *Early Ireland: An Introduction to Irish Prehistory*, Cambridge University Press, Cambridge.

Pezron, P.-Y. 1703, *Antiquité de la nation, et de langue des Celtes, autrement appellez Gaulois*, Paris.

Pezron, P.-Y. 1706, *The Antiquities of Nations, More particularly of the Celtae or*

Gauls, Taken to be Originally the same People as our Ancient Britains [sic], *Englished by Mr. Jones*, London.

Piggott, S. 1985a, *The Druids*, Thames & Hudson, London and New York.

Piggott, S. 1985b, *William Stukeley: An Eighteenth-Century Antiquary*, rev. edn, Thames & Hudson, London and New York.

Piggott, S. 1989, *Ancient Britons and the Antiquarian Imagination: Ideas from the Renaissance to the Regency*, Thames & Hudson, London and New York.

Pohl, W. 1997, 'Ethnic names and identities in the British Isles: a comparative perspective', in J. Hines (ed.), *The Anglo-Saxons, from the Migration Period to the Eighth Century: An Ethnographic Perspective*, Boydell Press, Woodbridge, pp. 7-40.

Powell, T.G.E. 1958, *The Celts*, new edn, Thames & Hudson, London.

Prebble, J. 1981, *The Lion in the North*, Penguin, Harmondsworth.

Raftery, B. 1994, *Pagan Celtic Ireland: The Enigma of the Irish Iron Age*, Thames & Hudson, London and New York.

Renfrew, C. 1987, *Archaeology and Language*, Penguin, Harmondsworth.

Renfrew, C. 1996, 'Prehistory and the identity of Europe, or, Don't let's be beastly to the Hungarians', in Graves-Brown *et al.* 1996, pp. 125-37.

Sharples, N. 1991, *Maiden Castle*, Batsford, London.

Sheehy, J. 1980, *The Rediscovery of Ireland's Past: The Celtic Revival 1830-1930*, Thames & Hudson, London and New York.

Stead, I.M. 1991, *Iron Age Cemeteries in East Yorkshire*, English Heritage, London.

Stead, I.M. 1997, *Celtic Art*, rev. edn, British Museum Press, London.

Trevor-Roper, H. 1983, 'The invention of tradition: the Highland tradition of Scotland', in E. Hobsbawm and T. Ranger (eds), *The Invention of Tradition*, Cambridge University Press, Cambridge, pp.15-41.

Webster, B. 1997, *Medieval Scotland: The Making of an Identity*, Macmillan, London and Basingstoke.

Webster, J., and Cooper, N. (eds), 1996, *Roman Imperialism: Post-colonial Perspectives*, Leicester Archaeology Monographs 3, Leicester.

Williams, G. 1985, *When was Wales?*, Penguin, Harmondsworth.

Williams, G. 1991, *The Welsh in Patagonia: The State and the Ethnic Community*, University of Wales Press, Cardiff.

Woodman, P. 1995, 'Who possesses Tara? Politics in archaeology in Ireland', in P. J. Ucko (ed.), *Theory in Archaeology: A World Perspective*, Routledge, London, pp. 278-97.

INDEX

ILLUSTRATION ACKNOWLEDGMENTS

Figs 1, 2, 9-14: drawings by Simon James. Figs 5-8: drawings by Karen
Hughes. Fig. 3: Irish Post Office/Irish Tourist Board; Fig. 4: Keith Jeffery/Sally
Visick Landscape.